Help us to pray

Help us to pray

John Thornbury

EVANGELICAL PRESS

EVANGELICAL PRESS
12 Wooler Street, Darlington, Co. Durham DL1 1RQ, England

© Evangelical Press 1991
First published 1991

British Library Cataloguing in Publication Data

Thornbury, John F.
  Help us to pray
  I. Title
  248.32

  ISBN 0 85234 286 1

By the same author:
God sent Revival

Printed and bound in Great Britain by the Bath Press, Avon.

Contents

Introduction

During the years of Jesus' ministry on earth, he was busily engaged in training his disciples for their work of proclaiming his gospel to the world. Although he often preached to the multitudes, most of his time was spent in intimate association with those he had chosen to do the work of his kingdom after his departure to heaven. Jesus was constantly teaching. On the grassy mountains of Galilee and Judea, along the dusty streets of Jerusalem, in the humble cottages where his disciples lived, in the marketplaces, and especially in the temple, the followers of Jesus listened in wonder as their Lord instructed them on his marvellous plan for their lives.

This book centres around an incident in the life of Jesus which focuses on his teachings pertaining to prayer. One of the disciples, probably acting as a spokesman for all the others, made a noteworthy and noble request: he asked the Saviour to teach him how to pray. 'Lord, teach us to pray, as John also taught his disciples,' he pleaded (Luke 11:1). Obviously this follower of Christ felt, on the one hand, a deep desire to pray, yet he was conscious of his own inadequacies and limitations in the all-important matter of prayer. He knew what he should do; he knew what he wanted to do — pray. But how should he go about it? How should he approach God? What words should he use?

Most of us today, who have been saved by the grace of Christ and desire to follow him, can identify with this disciple of long ago. We also long to have a deeper experience of communion with God. We know that the Bible promises rich blessings to those who have mastered the holy art of prayer, but how can we enter into these blessings? We love our heavenly Father and trust his Son who died for our sins on Calvary. But sinful creatures that we are, we feel woefully inadequate to come before the awesome throne of the sovereign God of heaven and earth. How often our attempts to pray have seemed so feeble! We even wonder if our prayers are being heard. How do we know if our prayers have pleased our Saviour and have been accepted?

It is in such a context that Jesus' teachings on prayer become so important. Immediately upon hearing this sincere request, 'Lord, teach us to pray,' Jesus began to instruct them on the various aspects of praying. Jesus comes before us in Luke 11:1-13 as the Master Teacher, the supreme instructor in the hows and wherefores of a dynamic prayer life. Here he gives a sort of digest of what he had taught and illustrated throughout his public ministry. The scope of his teachings here is very broad and very deep. He covers prayer in its manifold dimensions. He talks about prayer as worship, and prayer as petition. He talks about prayer as it relates to God and to our fellow man. He gives encouragement to pray. In fact, in order to make the essence of prayer as clear as possible, he even gives a model prayer or example for his people to use when they pray.

You might wish at this point to lay aside this book and pick up your Bible and read carefully and slowly our text, Luke 11:1-13. Read it as a devotional exercise, weighing each word and expression with intense concentration. I urge you after reading the text to go to God in prayer about the passage (in so far as you are able at this point). Ask the Lord to open up the rich meaning of the passage and use it as a doorway to a new experience of delightful communion with the Father. Pray that you will learn much about the goodness of the Lord in inviting you into his presence. Pray that this learning experience will not be just an intellectual exercise but that you will become, through this study, a true prayer warrior.

The Lord still wants us to 'learn of him' today, just as he did long ago as he walked the shores of Galilee. Physically speaking, we do not have the privilege of listening to his gracious voice or seeing his kind and gentle face, as did the disciples 2,000 years ago, but we have, instead, something better: we have his continuing presence through the Holy Spirit to awaken us, encourage us and strengthen us in prayer. Unlike the situation in Jesus' earthly ministry, we do not have to be in one particular location to learn from him. Jesus is bodily in heaven, where he will remain till his second coming. Wherever his people are, at home or abroad, on land, sea, or in the air, throughout the whole, wide world, at any time, they can sit at his feet and learn how to pray. Are you ready now for the lessons on prayer given by the Master Teacher himself?

1.
Pattern: Jesus, our example

'And it came to pass, as he was praying in a certain place...' (Luke 11:1).

Jesus, the Master Teacher, knew that the best way to teach was by example. And that was what he did. Everything he wanted the disciples to do — except of course in the duties which imply personal sinfulness (repentance, confession, etc.), or except in certain special relationships, such as marriage, Jesus did himself. He was not like his critics the Pharisees, who told people what to do but did not do it themselves (Matt. 23:3). The Saviour backed up his preaching and teaching by his behaviour.

Jesus Christ was both God and man. His mighty works which demonstrate his deity, such as creation (Col. 1:15-16), raising the dead (John 5:25) and judgement (John 5:27), are unique to him and obviously cannot be imitated by man. But as a human being Jesus set the perfect standard for human behaviour. In every aspect or dimension of his life, Jesus was flawless. He was a model child, for he submitted to his parents (Luke 2:51). He was exemplary as a citizen, for he admonished his followers to pay their lawful taxes (Matt. 22:21). He was a good neighbour, for he fed the hungry, healed the sick and encouraged the discouraged.

In his personal conduct Jesus the Messiah was conscientious, consistent and balanced. He stands alone as a man without a flaw. Even the greatest of the saints have blemishes in their character. Some seem to be very devoted to God, but show a callous indifference to the needs of their neighbours. Others are very people-oriented and humane, but show little regard for the vertical dimension of their lives, their relationship to God the Creator. With some, private virtue is all-important. They, to all appearances, pray and study much, but are inactive in the public realm of benevolence and generosity. With others, public service is what counts. They are busy doing and giving for others but spend little time, if any, in praise and worship. Not so with Jesus. He loved God supremely and also loved his fellow man, thus fulfilling the demands of God's law. He attended to all aspects of true virtue with the proper proportion and balance. He was a man of both devotion and service.

Looking at Jesus in prayer

Jesus was pre-eminently and consistently a man of prayer. Many of the occasions when he sought out a time of prayer are specially noted by the Gospel writers, Matthew, Mark, Luke and John. Some of his actual prayers are recorded, such as when he gave thanks to the Father in Matthew 11:25-26, and his intercessory prayer in John 17.

We learn a few interesting details about Jesus' prayer life from Mark's first reference to Jesus praying: 'Now in the morning, having risen a long while before daylight, he went out and departed to a solitary place, and there he prayed' (Mark 1:35). Here we learn that personal devotion and prayer were a priority with Jesus. This is seen in the fact that he set aside the best part of the day for communion with God. On this occasion Jesus sought God early in the morning, and we have no reason to believe that this was anything unusual.

Many people find that the early morning hours, long before the busy activities of the day begin, are an excellent time to set aside for devotional times. It is usually quiet. The chances are that the phone will not be ringing and that the noise level on the streets outside will not be as high as at other times. Also many believers find that their minds are more alert in the morning, so that they are able to dedicate the very best time of the day to spiritual matters. The important thing to keep in mind is that we should select a time during which we are the most disposed to mental and spiritual labours. The Christian who is a 'slow starter' and who tends to be dull early in the day, becoming more mentally active as the day progresses, may need to reserve a prayer time later in the evening before retiring. *Let us*, in any case, *give our best times to our Saviour*. Mark 1:35 tells us that Jesus sought a place *where he could be alone* for prayer.

Jesus prayed before important events

We are particularly told how Jesus spent time in prayer before certain momentous occasions in his life. For example, Luke tells us that before he selected the twelve disciples, the group who would form the inner core of his followers, he spent the entire night in prayer (Luke 6:12). 'When it was day,' we are told, 'he called his disciples to him; and from them he chose twelve whom he also named apostles' (v. 13). Think for a moment what an important time this was for the Lord. The twelve apostles were the ones selected by God, along with the Old Testament prophets, to be the foundation of the Christian church. They were specially equipped and commissioned to give forth the Word of God to the early Christians and train them in the teachings of Jesus. Some of them, such as Peter and John, were endowed with supernatural guidance so they could write inspired Scripture. They were destined to have their names inscribed on the walls of the New Jerusalem (Rev. 21:14), an honour that is no doubt as great as it is mysterious.

Jesus did not conduct an all-night prayer vigil because of any indecision or perplexity as to whom he should choose. Nor was he doubtful as to what successes or failures these men would have as they embarked on their appointed mission. He not only knew ahead of time the power Peter would have as a preacher and the wonderful gifts John would exercise as a writer, but he also knew that one of his disciples was a 'devil' and would betray him (John 6:64,70). The time Jesus spent in prayer was a part of his preparatory work in laying well the foundations of his kingdom. He prayed for his disciples ahead of time, knowing full well what difficulties they would have as they went forth with his message.

How important it is that Christ's people follow his example in praying before important occasions in their lives! Life-changing events such as the first day in school, a new job, marriage, baptism, joining the church, or an important speech, are examples of times when we need to seek God's help earnestly. And, unlike our all-knowing Lord, we do *not* know what the outcome of our decisions will be.

Life affords countless situations where we need wisdom from God in decision-making. Let us suppose, for example, that a firm has entrusted you with the responsibility of recruiting staff. There are dozens of applicants for a couple of positions. Careers, livelihoods and people's feelings are all at stake. Two fortunate people will be gladdened by your decision, but many others will be sent away disappointed. The welfare of the business is in the balance. A wise choice may guarantee a bright future for the business, which will in turn provide employment for many other people at some time. On the other hand, if the wrong people are appointed, the entire venture may be jeopardized, not to mention the personal agony you may face in having to dismiss someone. Anyone who is in such a situation needs to pray much before making the necessary choices.

Jesus prayed before his suffering and death

We also find our Lord praying when he was about to face a time of trial and suffering. All four Gospels give an account of his agonizing time of prayer on the Mount of Olives before his arrest, trial and crucifixion. As the dreadful hour approached when he was to give himself up to the treacherous Judas, he said to the disciples, 'Sit here while I pray' (Mark 14:32). Having selected Peter, James and John to share this traumatic moment, he began, we are told, to be 'troubled and deeply distressed' (v. 33). Crushed under the weight of the unimaginable pain he was soon to endure, he sought the encouragement and solace of his disciples, but all in vain. 'Stay here and watch,' he urged (v. 34), but when he returned he found them sleeping. 'Watch and pray,' he admonished, 'lest you enter into temptation. The spirit truly is ready, but the flesh is weak' (v. 38).

If the Son of God, who was not only the perfect man but also God incarnate, found it necessary to engage in prayer before a time of suffering, how much more necessary is it for all of us! Afflictions, whether they be physical, mental, or spiritual, bring out both the best and the worst in human nature. They drive some people to God, but others choose to turn away from him when they strike. Some are able to submit meekly to God's will; others complain against God's providence or even rail against him in anger. Some come through trials stronger in faith and purged from harmful attitudes and practices; others are made bitter and become hopelessly hardened. Nothing tests a person's character like a severe trial. So it is easy to see that we need to pray, and pray earnestly, when we anticipate a time of trial, as well as during and after a trial.

Jesus prayed for others

What a marvellous example Jesus gives to us for intercessory prayer! There is no doubt that for the Saviour prayer was a part of his life of devotion and worship of his Father, who had sent him. His prayers were a means of gaining wisdom and strength as one who came to do the will of God (John 4:34; 17:1-5). But as the great High Priest he came not only to offer himself as a sacrifice for sin, which he did by dying on the cross, but also to intercede on behalf of others. Of course his greatest recorded prayer is the prayer for the disciples in John 17:6-26. In this prayer Jesus covered the whole range of interests and concerns that his people have. He prays for their unity, sanctification and preservation.

Jesus' prayers were for all his chosen ones in general, yet they were also for each one in particular. In Luke 22:31-34 Jesus warned Peter that he was the object of Satan's temptation. How comforting must have been these words of reassurance: 'But I have prayed for you, that your faith should not fail.' Two of Jesus' disciples, Judas and Peter, demonstrated moral weakness and both were unfaithful. Judas betrayed Jesus to his enemies and Peter denied him before a hostile crowd. Why did Peter not fall totally away and become an apostate like Judas? The only difference was the sovereign intercession of the Saviour. Judas was a devil and his doom was foreknown by the Saviour. But Peter was a true disciple and though he had to learn a terrible lesson about his own weakness through his fall, Jesus' prayers upheld him.

The Christian cannot share in the special role Jesus had as the God-man, whose intercessory work is a part of redemption. But believers are priests and can intercede on behalf of others. It has been said that a prophet speaks to people on behalf of God and the priest speaks to God on behalf of the people. Certainly one function of a priest is to invoke the blessings of God upon his fellow men (see Gen.14:19). The believer, as a part of God's 'royal priesthood' (1 Peter 2:9) can and should, like his Lord and Master Jesus, pray for others. Those prayers should not only include members of his or her immediate family, but brothers and sisters in the Christian faith, and also even his enemies (Matt. 5:44). Supplications and prayers should be offered to God for public officials so that the church can live peaceable lives (1 Tim. 2:1-2). (An excellent model for intercessory prayer is found in 1 Samuel 12:22-23.)

There is far too little intercessory prayer among believers today. At best life is a constant series of upsets and turmoils in our relationships with others. In the home, at work and in the church, we are ever aware not only of our own problems but of those of others. When other people fail it seems to be a human tendency for people to react with harshness, anger and even needless gossip. Some run to their close friends for sympathy when there is a disagreement in the home or the church. Phone conversations and discussions on the street, often in a fretful spirit, like the gusts of wind blowing through a burning field, only serve to make matters worse. How much better, when someone has hurt us or has strayed from the path of obedience, to go directly to God and pray for the people involved! This certainly is at the least the *first* course of action.

Our church has recently printed a directory containing a picture of each of the family units in our fellowship. As I looked over pages of the various people I immediately saw that this directory can be a powerful tool for prayer. My wife and I have resolved to pray specifically for at least one family each day. We will pray for that elderly person who recently has had financial difficulties. We will pray for that young man who has gone off to college and is making choices which will drastically affect his life. We will pray for the lady whose husband was recently taken from her. We will pray for the young couple whose precious little girl has been constantly ill. All of us need to have longer prayer lists.

For many years our church has had in place a 'prayer and information chain' consisting of several dozens of families. When there is an emergency in our fellowship a call can be received in the church office and in a few moments many people are aware of the need and are praying about the matter. We do not have the infinite knowledge of Jesus to pray for the vast host that makes up his mystical body. But we all have a circle of friends and acquaintances who need intercessory prayer. We can emulate Paul, who assured the Roman Christians, 'God is my witness, whom I serve with my spirit in the gospel of his Son, that without ceasing I make mention of you always in my prayers' (Rom.1:9). We often think of Paul as the great missionary, or the great theologian, but here we see perhaps his greatest virtue: he was a mighty intercessor. Throughout his epistles he reveals the heart of a great shepherd for all who had been saved as a result of his preaching.

Jesus prayed with submission

Not only is Jesus Christ a perfect model for the prayer life of the Christian in the situations and subjects of his prayers, but he also sets the ideal standard in his attitude in prayer. Although he prayed with absolute confidence and faith in his heavenly Father, Jesus also prayed with total submission to the Father's will. Hebrews 5:7-8 says of the Saviour, 'Who in the days of his flesh, when he had offered up prayers and supplications, with vehement cries and tears to him who was able to save him from death, and was heard because of his godly fear, though he was a Son, yet he learned obedience by the things which he suffered.' The Gospels record how Jesus' human nature recoiled from the terrible sufferings he faced as he appproached his death on Calvary. In agony he cried out, 'Father, if it is your will, remove this cup from me' (Luke 22:42). Yet without hesitation, he totally yielded his own human desires to God's preordained plan. 'Nevertheless,' he continued, 'not my will, but yours, be done.' There was no quarrelling with God's purpose, or resentment of the painful work he had to do. His face was set like a flint to do the will of God. He was totally submitted to the all-wise programme of his Father. Though a Son, he learned obedience by the things he suffered.

God expects his people freely and honestly to share their needs with him. He wants us to believe as we pray — that he is willing and able to answer us. God does not honour faithless praying (James 1:6-7). But a fretful, complaining spirit is foreign to the teachings of the gospel. When we come to God in prayer we do not come making demands but humbly beseeching him. It ill becomes sinful creatures to question the wisdom of the almighty God. 'Not my will, but yours be done,' should be words frequently upon our lips. Jesus submitted his will to that of the Father. Why should we hesitate to do so?

In every way Jesus' life of prayer is worthy of emulation on the part of his people. His prayers were worshipful, sincere, earnest and constant. As directed to God they were full of faith and submission. As offered on behalf of men, they were characterized by infinite tenderness and compassion.

The Saviour's frequent admonition to his disciples to 'Follow me' is especially applicable in the all-important work of prayer. To follow Jesus means to pray frequently, pray earnestly and pray successfully. The steps of Jesus lead us to the quiet place where, undisturbed by the distractions of worldly affairs, we can commune with our heavenly Father. If we are like our Lord and Master we will be a compassionate people who bear the needs of others to God. The prayers of Jesus, the great loving Shepherd, have brought down all the spiritual blessings his people enjoy. Acting under his guidance and inspired by his example, we who know him can also be channels of blessing to those around us.

2.
Privilege: the opportunity of prayer

'So he said to them, "When you pray. . ."' (Luke 11:2).

It is clear that Jesus Christ anticipated that his disciples would be praying men. In fact he took it for granted that talking to God would be a basic, integral part of their lives as his followers. He did not impose prayer upon them as though it were some difficult or irksome task. Rather Jesus assumed that prayer is as pleasurable as it is necessary, as rewarding as it is obligatory.

The privilege of prayer is often taken for granted. Most of us would consider it a marvellous honour to be invited to spend an evening in the company of some notable person, such as the Prime Minister of Britain or the President of the United States. A man once showed me a letter he had received inviting him to a political reception at which President George Bush was to speak. His face beamed with pride as he produced the document certifying his place at this important occasion. Yet how insignificant is such an honour in comparison with the privilege of talking personally to the Lord of glory! To go to him, knowing that he hears and responds to our prayers is, when we consider it, an unbelievable opportunity.

The God to whom we pray

Who is the God with whom Jesus expected his disciples to communicate in prayer? What is he like? After all, prayer is worthless unless it has the right object. Although communication with a 'higher power' is inherent in all religions, how vastly different are their concepts of God! Peoples of the ancient civilizations worshipped the sun and the moon and a variety of idols made of wood, stone and precious metals. Hinduism has millions of gods which have evolved through successive generations, none of whom is able to have a dynamic personal relationship with the worshipper. Certain tribes of Africa give their devotion to demon spirits, whom they seek to appease by torturous rituals. The New Age movement, which is sweeping across the Western world, holds forth the promise that man himself can attain to a godlike status, thus encouraging self-worship.

Jesus Christ's concept of God and of devotion to him cannot be separated from his historical and spiritual roots. He was a Jew, whose teachings were based upon the theological concepts of the nation of Israel, as set forth in the Old Testament Scriptures. Look on almost any page in the Old Testament and you see a picture of an almighty God of awesome glory, totally unlike any of the other deities which were worshipped by the nations of antiquity. These writings reveal a God who demands supreme affection and praise from his creatures. Indeed not only is such worship commanded, but such books as the Psalms of David demonstrate that this great God inspires and elicits from his subjects passionate devotion. David said,

'As the deer pants for the water brooks,
So pants my soul for you, O God.
My soul thirsts for God, for the living God.
When shall I come and appear before God?'

(Ps. 42:1-2).

Several characteristics of the God whom Jesus Christ proclaimed are relevant as we consider the meaning of prayer. For one thing, the God of the Hebrews is *solitary*. The Israelites, alone of all the nations of past ages, taught that there is only one true and living God. The surrounding peoples, both the smaller tribes such as the Philistines and the Hittites, and the larger and more powerful kingdoms such as the Babylonians, the Greeks and the Romans, had many gods. There were gods of war and peace, gods of earth and nature, gods of heaven and hell and gods who symbolized reproduction. They were cruel, capricious, lustful and selfish, just like the people who invented them. But the God of the Old Testament is represented as holy, just, merciful and long-suffering. Such a God Jesus served and proclaimed to the world of his day.

The God of the Hebrews is not only solitary, but also *personal*.

Not everyone believes in a personal God. To many people God is synonymous with the universe, that is, with everything. They regard God as having reality, but only as a nebulous flux, or the spirit that animates the sum total of all existence. One might have a vague feeling of respect for such a 'spirit', or the awesomeness of the universe might cause someone, in a moment of inspiration, to reflect with deep feelings of respect. But a person would hardly pray to a god who is simply the sum total of everything. As a true Hebrew, however, Jesus taught that God is 'out there' as a living, personal, conscious and active being. Jesus talked to him and heard him speak in response. Jesus claimed to have been sent by him (John 4:34) and declared his intention to return to him (John 16:10). The God of Jesus was a God who could be known personally and loved intimately.

The sovereign God preached by Jesus was not only personal, but also *spiritual*. Jesus said to a woman of Samaria, 'God is Spirit, and those who worship him must worship in spirit and truth' (John 4:24). Jesus is teaching here that God is an immaterial being — invisible, intangible and indestructible. He is not matter and is not dependent upon matter. He is pure spirit. The Hebrews were not only forbidden to make or worship any kind of physical idol, but in the second of the Ten Commandments they were told that the true God was not to be adored under any physical representation (Exod. 20:4-6). It is very difficult, if not impossible, for a human being to worship *before* something and not worship the thing itself. For this reason God forbade Israel to create any material object to symbolize him. Jesus taught that the true God is to be worshipped spiritually, that is with the mind and the heart. Man's communication with him is to be inward and personal, not through veneration of a created image.

Jesus' God was also *all-powerful*. He creates, sustains and controls the physical universe and all that is in it. To Jesus, the world is God's creation (Mark 13:19). He is the God who feeds the birds, designs the beautiful flowers and dresses the fields with green grass (Matt. 6:26-30). He is a God who could, if he wishes, turn stones into people (Matt. 3:9). He is a God who gives life, raises the dead and can destroy soul and body in hell (John 5:21; Matt. 10:28). He is a God who reveals himself to those who humbly seek him, but hides the truth from the arrogant (Matt. 11:25).

Certainly if prayer is to be meaningful it must be directed to a God who has all power and dominion. People are accustomed to conceiving of prayer as seeking blessings from God, and rightly so. Prayer means asking God to change circumstances, change hearts, direct the events of time and history — in short to intervene in our lives and the course of affairs on this earth. But it would be utterly foolish to ask God to do this if he were unable to do it.

Think with me for a moment. Would you ask a three-year-old toddler to repair the engine in your car? Would you recruit a cripple to play in a soccer match? Would you ask a mentally retarded person to explain to you the formulas of Euclid or Einstein's theory of relativity? Obviously not. A person with normal intelligence solicits help only from those who are competent actually to meet the need. Yet there are people today who are totally inconsistent on the matter of God's power and prayer. Some modern theologians openly proclaim the 'finiteness' of God, and say that his power is limited. Others, anxious to relieve God of any responsibility for human pain, say that he has no control over natural disasters and accidents. Yet, strangely, such people constantly solicit prayer for God's protection when they travel or are engaged in a risky enterprise. But we need not worry that the true God has any such limitations. The God of the Bible, the Father to whom Jesus led people to direct their petitions, can answer prayer, because he really does have sovereign control over all people and events.

Finally, the God of the Hebrews, whom Jesus proclaimed and served, is *all-knowing*. Following in the tradition of such prophets as Isaiah, who spoke of God as 'declaring the end from the beginning, and from ancient times things that are not yet done' (Isa. 46:10), Jesus of Nazareth led his disciples to trust in a God who has all knowledge. He knows what is going to happen in the future (Mark 13:32). He is perfectly aware of all the needs of his children, even before they ask him (Matt. 6:8). In fact, God even knows the number of the constantly changing hairs of the human scalp (Matt. 10:30).

What an encouraging truth the omniscience of God is! What a tremendous incentive to prayer! Just think, no matter what we are praying about, regardless of how mysterious or difficult it may be, the Lord knows all about it. He knows the cause of the situation, the complexities of the situation and the solution to the situation.

A friend of mine, named Jim, relates this interesting incident which illustrates the knowledge as well as the goodness of God. During his teen years he was a bright student in school, active in all kinds of sports. He had everything going for him. Unfortunately, however, he contracted rheumatic fever and lay in a coma for several weeks. His father was a doctor and knew the potential seriousness of the situation. This disease often has permanent negative consequences, such as heart disease. The doctor called for the family and personal friends and said that there was nothing he could do. A pastor who was present recommended that they pray. Jim's father said he did not know how to pray. But they did pray and the next day Jim began to come out of his coma. He overheard the doctor say, however, that he had a leak in his heart and if he ever recovered at all he would be an invalid for the rest of his life. He would never be able to be active again.

Jim was crushed by the news he had heard. He had been converted earlier at a youth camp and he began to seek help from God himself. He even 'bargained' with God, promising that he would consecrate his life wholly to him if he were healed. In the next few weeks he was given the best medical treatment available and kept under careful observation. To make a long story short, Jim was completely cured and lived to be a successful businessman. He also became active once again in athletics and graduated with honours. He eventually went to seminary and became a pastor.

There is no question that the prayers for Jim were answered by a God who knew all about his situation. God knew all about the rheumatic fever long before it took place. He planned that the pastor and other friends should pray for him. In fact God knew even from eternity that this very disease would develop in the modern world and in his infinite goodness he provided the medical facilities and the technical help that he knew would be conducive to Jim's recovery. Never mind that the scientists and physicians who were involved may not have known that an almighty hand was directing them. God was supervising the investigations and the discoveries just the same. Sometimes God uses as instruments even those who do not give him the glory.

God's omniscience and power is also seen in his answering prayers for the conversion of sinners. In a gospel tract entitled *From the Chains of Alcoholism to the Yoke of Christ*, Morris tells about his remarkable conversion experience. He was for eighteen years an alcoholic and lived a miserable existence. Once in a drunken stupor he took a handful of sleeping pills with the thought that when he woke up he would be O.K., and if not 'it really did not matter'. His wife found him and called for the doctors to come. He did recover but for a while the combination of drugs and beer caused violent shocks in his body.

In the providence of God a man working with him in a factory shared with him the gospel of Christ. He showed him in the Bible about man's sin and God's remedy, the redemptive work of Christ. Morris began to ask God for forgiveness for his sins and even started having prayer with his family, but kept up his drinking. He hid his beer in the pantry and drank on the sly. The Christian who had been seeking to help him told him one day that his family would pray for him. 'That really hit home to my heart. I could not understand why anyone would have enough compassion on a wretch like me to be that concerned.' That night he knew he would need more drink.

Morris began to come to our church and listen to the gospel. His heart was in awful torment as he struggled with the conflicting desires for drink and the prickings of his conscience. One night, after reading his Bible, he dropped on his knees and cried out to God saying, 'O Lord God in heaven, if I'm not saved, please, please save me!' Then he sat down to listen to a gospel record with the song, 'Why should he love me so?' and also 'There's room at the cross for you.' 'When I heard those words,' he says, 'I caught a glimpse of Jesus and my heart broke. It was then and there that I fell in love with him . . . I know from experience that there is no sin too great for Christ to forgive, and no habit too strong for him to break.'

The conversion of Morris demonstrates not only the power but the omniscience of God. God knew all about the awful effects strong drink would have over his mind and body. He knew that he needed someone to share the gospel with him, thus he providentially placed a man near him at work to witness to him. In his goodness God gave him a Christian wife to pray for him. He guided Morris to our church to hear the gospel and led him to purchase a gospel record that was faithful to the redemptive work of Christ.

These examples illustrate the two glorious attributes of God, his omnipotence and omniscience. Putting them together we have a dynamic basis for prayer. No situation is too difficult or complicated for him. In the words of Paul, God is 'able to do exceedingly abundantly above all that we ask or think according to the power that works in us' (Eph. 3:20). We do indeed have a great and glorious God who is able and willing to answer prayer.

All men should seek the Lord

The Bible, as well as our own reasoning, leads us to believe that there is one true and living God. This is the God proclaimed by the Hebrew prophets, Jesus Christ and his apostles. He has made all things that exist, including all people who live on earth. In him alone are found true happiness and salvation. He has made us in his image, with the powers of thought and choice. We are all responsible to love and serve him. But service begins by prayer — by seeking God's face and asking his forgiveness through the shed blood of his Son. Prayer, therefore, is a universal duty. All men ought to pray.

This is what Jesus Christ taught. 'Men,' he said, 'ought always to pray and not lose heart' (Luke 18:1). How easy it is for people who are walking the road of life, which is sometimes long and difficult, to 'lose heart'! A formidable assortment of woes press upon us. Disease, old age, poverty, loneliness, guilt, bereavement and war are all familiar realities in this world. Yet what do people do when troubles come? Some become angry and violent and turn to a life of crime. Some worry themselves into a state of nervous exhaustion and have to receive medical attention. Some try to drown their sorrows in drug or alcohol addiction. But others turn to the One who can really help them, the God of heaven and earth.

People should pray to God not just because he can help them, but because *he is worthy of their praise and worship*. Someone has said, 'Where all is, there all should be.' All is in God. All life and power are in him. All truth and justice are in him. All mercy and grace are in him. Since all these things are in God, then every person, indeed every intelligent creature (angels included) should bow before his throne in humble dependence and faith.

God commands all the peoples of the world to seek him in faith and prayer: 'Seek the Lord while he may be found, call upon him while he is near' (Isa. 55:6). This is a command to all men and nations in all times and places. To seek God means to enquire as to who God is and what he is like. It means to search his Word, the Bible, to find out what his requirements are and what we are to do. It means to pray, confess our sins and receive his gospel. Since God has revealed himself through his Son Jesus Christ it means to acknowledge Jesus as the Lord and Saviour and submit to his rule. God sent Christ to be a substitute for sinners. On a Roman cross outside of Jerusalem, 2,000 years ago, Jesus died to pay the debt of sin. Only by coming to him and accepting him as a crucified, buried and risen Saviour can anyone find forgiveness and salvation. Have you sought God through his Son Jesus?

Although God deserves our worship and praise, and although true salvation and assurance can be found in him alone, the fact is that multitudes, yes even the majority, do not pray. They go about their busy lives living as though there were no God. They pay no attention to his clear call from the physical universe which loudly declares his existence. They ignore God's Word, the Bible, and often despise the people who proclaim it. They never get on their knees and talk to the God who made them. J. C. Ryle laments the callous attitude of many in his fine little book, *A Call to Prayer:* 'I believe that thousands never utter a word of prayer at all. They eat. They drink. They sleep. They rise. They go forth to their labour. They return to their homes. They breathe God's air. They see God's sun. They walk on God's earth. They enjoy God's mercies . . . But they never speak to God. They live like the beasts that perish. They behave like creatures without souls.' How sad, but how true!

3.

Position: the believer's relationship to God

'When you pray, say: Our Father in heaven' (Luke 11:2).

All men ought to pray, but relatively few do. The truth is that the human race is in a state of rebellion against the Creator and all men tend by nature to run from God. Generally speaking, their interests are in the achievements, pleasures and honours of this world. To many people calling on God seems foolish, since they feel that they are able to make it on their own. They are confident that with enough determination, patience and perseverance, they can survive.

To some extent the self-sufficiency and vain self-confidence so prevalent today are supported by the great emphasis placed on self-esteem and positive thinking. Thousands today pay a lot of money to hear psychologists and self-motivation experts pour into their brains the idea that 'The sky is the limit,' in so far as what they can accomplish. Even some ministers aid and abet the vanity of the public by stressing over and over again the potential of the individual and the power of the human will. With this kind of emphasis, is it any wonder that few feel a need to humble themselves and seek help from God? The sad thing is that, although there is an element of truth in positive thinking, much of this emphasis is unrealistic. Often victims of misfortune find themselves crushed beneath the disappointments of life and are left bitter and disappointed when they discover that they need more than a positive mental attitude.

Scepticism abounds in our world, as it always has done, about the value of prayer. Some even ridicule those who depend on a sovereign God for help and ascribe all the blessings of life to him. I heard a story about a farmer who ventured into a big city and took a seat at a table in a restaurant, along with his wife and several children. At home it was his custom to give thanks to his God for providing the meal, so he felt no need to deviate from his usual practice on this occasion. A few ruffians were seated nearby and noted with some scorn that this group of plain-looking people were praying. When they finished one rude fellow blurted out in a sarcastic tone, 'Say, man, does everyone out in the hills duck their heads before they eat?' The farmer flushed briefly, and then replied firmly, 'No sir, the hogs don't, they just dive in.' How sad that vast multitudes drink in the blessings of God, yet never stop to acknowledge their source!

The truth is that all of us, the writer included, tend to rely on our own human strength to struggle along until we learn again how helpless we are and how dependent on God. Unfortunately turning to God is, even for many who wear the name of Christian, a last resort.

All men are not God's children

Why is it that people try with all their might to avoid a friendly relationship with their Creator? Why is it that they resort to any stratagem to escape the presence of the God who calls to them? Why is it that men so easily, so carelessly, forsake the only true source of peace for their souls? The answer is to be found in the true spiritual condition of mankind. The Bible tells us that all are by nature fallen, sinful, totally depraved creatures. They do not love God, seek God, or want God. They are in fact — I am aware of how harsh this sounds, but it is true — enemies of God. The Scriptures tell us that apart from God's grace all men are children of the devil. It is truly Satan, the supernatural but fallen spirit who wages war against God's kingdom, who dupes poor blinded people into believing that they can manage all right without faith and prayer.

'Children of the devil?', I hear someone saying. How awful to speak so negatively of many of the noble people who live on our earth! How judgemental! How primitive, in this enlightened and tolerant age to classify some as belonging to the devil! Yet Jesus Christ himself brought just such a cutting charge against people of his own day and, believe it or not, they were religious people at that! Listen to his stinging words: 'You are of your father the devil, and the desires of your father you want to do' (John 8:44). These words were spoken to those who had rejected his claims and were opposing his ministry.

But wait, before we are too quick to condemn those who fell under such a scathing denunciation from the Lord, let us pause to ponder the fact that *all* who have not turned to God in saving repentance and faith are the children of the devil. The truth is that either we are children of God by faith, or we are the children of the devil by unbelief. There is no middle ground. There is no twilight zone of moral and spiritual neutrality. There is no straddling the line of demarcation between the kingdoms of darkness and light. Jesus himself said, 'He who is not with me is against me' (Luke 11:23). We either love God or hate him. We either trust him or place our faith in something else. We either submit to God or are enemies of his kingdom and righteousness.

I am aware that it is customary in our day to blur the sharp distinction between believers and unbelievers. It is popular in many religious circles to accept blandly as true Christians all who profess any kind of religious faith. It is considered mean-spirited to question the authenticity of anyone, no matter how inconsistent his or her life may be with the biblical standard of discipleship. We often hear such statements as, 'As long as people are sincere and strive to be good, we should not judge them.' Yet the Bible warns that not all who say, 'Lord, Lord,' shall enter the kingdom of God, but those who do God's will (Matt. 7:21).

Nothwithstanding the clear teaching of Scripture that some are children of God and some are not, many believe in what has been called the 'fatherhood of God and the brotherhood of man'. This view was taught by the German theologian Albrecht Ritschl and mediated to Great Britain and America by Adolf Von Harnack. These men denied the deity of Christ and taught that to be truly Christian is simply to follow the example of Jesus of Nazareth, who embodied the best and noblest in human nature. According to these theologians, one need not be converted in order to be a child of God. All men are already God's children by creation. The purpose of the church is simply to announce the good news that we are all brothers, looking up to the same loving Father of us all. Even though the people of earth do not realize it, God loves and accepts them and owns them as his sons.

How far removed this teaching of the fatherhood of God and brotherhood of man is from the Scriptures! Although this is a concept that is very soothing and very comfortable to the masses of ignorant people, it is contrary to the teachings of Christ. Jesus Christ said plainly that in order to enter the kingdom of God one must be 'born again' (John 3:3). He assured the people of his day that they would have to be converted and become humble, like little children, in order to share in the blessings of salvation (Matt. 18:3). John the Baptist, a prophet who introduced Christ to the world, proclaimed that those who do not believe on Jesus as the Son of God abide under the wrath of God (John 3:36). There is no fuzzy, sentimental neutralism here. Let us make no mistake about it. We need to be clear in our minds on this point. All are not the children of God. All are not saved. All are not Christians.

Although it is outside the main intention of our study on prayer to discuss the way of salvation here, perhaps it might be well to note that a person becomes a Christian by experiencing a marvellous, supernatural change. From God's standpoint it is a *birth*, a bringing forth of new life in the soul. From the human standpoint it is *conversion,* a 'turning around' from a life of selfishness and sin to a life of trust in Christ and submission to his will. The negative side of conversion is repentance, which means acknowledging and confessing sin. This means sincerely regretting past sinful conduct and resolving to live differently. The positive side of conversion is faith, which involves an acceptance of the truth of the gospel about Christ and a hearty trust in him alone for salvation. Jesus himself exhorted the people of Galilee, 'Repent, and believe in the gospel' (Mark 1:15).

Repentance and faith go together. A coin does not have one side but two. So the experience of conversion has two sides: turning from sin and turning to Christ. One cannot repent without believing, and one cannot believe without repenting. Becoming a Christian is something like entering a house. One must *leave* the outside and *enter* the inside. One leaves by entering and enters by leaving. So becoming a believer means to leave the world of darkness and sin and enter God's blessed abode of love and grace.

When a person genuinely accepts God's claims in the gospel and places his faith in Christ's death and righteousness to save him, he becomes a child of God. He now has a new nature, a new motive in life and a new family. He is walking a new road, the 'straight and narrow' way of obedience to his heavenly Father. He has a new destiny, heaven, where he will dwell for ever in the blessed presence of God.

It is true that all men are obliged by virtue of their relationship to their Creator to call on God in prayer. But until a person has received the gospel and become God's child, he does not have a relationship with God entitling him to a life of fellowship with God in prayer. How can God entertain with favour those who are his enemies? How can he share an intimate fellowship with people who are unreconciled to him? How can he welcome into his presence those who despise his Son?

It is only through the mediation of Jesus Christ that we can come into the presence of a holy God. Only through the peace that he has wrought on Calvary can we have fellowship with the Father. Jesus said, 'I am the way, the truth, and the life. No one comes to the Father except through me' (John 14:6). Paul, writing in 1 Timothy 2:5 says, 'For there is one God and one Mediator between God and men, the man Christ Jesus.' If Christ is the only way to God, then those who do not receive him are not on the right way; they are lost. If Christ is the sole mediator between God and man, anyone who seeks to approach God except by virtue of his merits cannot expect to be received. Let us settle the matter once and for all. Salvation, with all its attendant blessings, such as forgiveness of sin and entitlement to eternal glory in heaven, is *through Jesus Christ alone*, plus nothing and minus nothing. Outside of Christ there is nothing but judgement and hell.

Privileges of sonship

Clearly Jesus is using a figure of speech here when he tells his disciples that God is their Father. Jesus taught his disciples in language they could understand. He drew illustrations from life situations with which they were familiar. The parables he gave were taken from manners and customs characteristic of his native country and culture. For example, he taught that his mission to earth to save sinners is like that of a shepherd who goes out to seek a sheep which has strayed from the fold. Preaching the gospel is like sowing seed in a field. Accountability to God for our opportunities and gifts is like the responsibility of a steward to whom money has been committed for investment.

The father-child relationship is one of the most common and familiar with which human beings are accustomed. Frequently the first words an infant utters are some simple syllables meaning 'daddy'. It is a word which, in normal circumstances, denotes love, companionship, guidance and protection. It speaks of a tender, intimate and special relationship.

The term 'father' has a special meaning to me personally. I recall when I was a child of about thirteen or fourteen my father had taken me out into a field to play baseball with me. In the game of baseball one player hits a ball and another catches it. On this particular day, my father, who was then in his mid-thirties, was throwing the ball up, smacking it with his bat, and I was trying to catch it with my fielder's glove. Suddenly I noticed that a man, who was a very prominent citizen in the community in fact, had driven up to the edge of the road and was watching very intently. Finally he stepped out of the car and said to my father in my hearing, 'If more dads would do like you, Jeff, there would be fewer juvenile delinquents.' At the time I did not know the meaning of 'delinquent'. But I made it my business to find out. At the end of this day I had learned two things: I learned what a delinquent was, and I learned that I would never, never, become one if I could possibly help it, simply out of love and respect for my father.

I was more fortunate than many children. Regrettably, some grow up with a negative image of father. (This seems to be an increasingly common problem in our day.) To many young girls and boys the word 'father' brings feelings of terror or repulsion. They picture in their minds a man who is seldom around, and when he is at home he is either indifferent to them or downright cruel. They may visualize a man staggering in late at night and pounding mercilessly on their mother. But it was not so with me. I was blessed with a good father. He had my best interests in mind. He cared. I knew that whatever he had was at my disposal if I needed it. He always had time to listen if I had a problem. Most of all, he prayed for me.

This positive image of God as Father is what Jesus Christ had in mind. He was setting forth his Father, the one who loved him and sent him into the world to be the Redeemer, as a loving, kind, gracious, patient, accessible and faithful parent. He wishes the disciples to know that their God is not one who is afar off, reigning in some distant place with no regard for their needs or concerns. He is a God who has begotten them. They belong to him. He is vitally interested in them. He is ready, willing and anxious to listen to their prayers.

Jesus Christ set forth in seminal form the great doctrine of God's fatherly care of his children under the New Covenant. He lays a foundation which is developed and applied at length in the teachings of the epistles. Such books as Romans, Galatians and John's epistles expound in great detail the glorious privilege of being a son of God. It is a privilege of incredible honour, glory and power. As the old hymn puts it,

My father is rich in houses and lands,
He holdeth the wealth of the world in his hands.
Of rubies, of diamonds, of silver and gold,
His coffers are full, he has riches untold.

I'm a child of the King, a child of the King.
With Jesus my Saviour, I'm a child of the King.

Just think, a Christian is a child of the King — not just some earthly sovereign who, however powerful and wealthy, is frail, limited and mortal. But the Christian is the child of the glorious God of heaven, who spoke the worlds into being and holds the universe in the palm of his hand. And the marvellous thing is that this is a position that every believer has, whatever his position down here on earth may be. He may be in the depths of poverty, grovelling in squalor and eking out a bare existence, but in the spiritual world he is fabulously wealthy, for God is his Father. He may for a while be forsaken by his neighbours, friends, or even his own family, yet he is the object of a love that can never fail, the love of the unchanging God. He may be a victim of terrible persecution for his faith and be forced to sit in some lonely cell, scarcely able to see the light of day, yet as a member of God's family he is under the patient care of a God who understands every hurt and never, never forgets. Truly, as David said so graphically, 'As a father pities his children, so the Lord pities those who fear him' (Ps. 103:13). What a glorious privilege to be a child of God! What an exalted position!

It lies outside the compass of this study to deal at length with the rich teachings of the New Testament on the theme of justification by faith and the associate truth of adoption. But one privilege of sonship is so germane to the whole subject of prayer that it cannot be passed over. I am speaking of the marvellous privilege of *access into the presence of our heavenly Father*. This is expounded in many places in the New Testament, but nowhere more powerfully than by Paul in Ephesians 3:11-12. He refers here to God's eternal purpose, which assures us of security in Christ's redemption, 'in whom' (referring to Jesus Christ) 'we have boldness and access with confidence through faith in him'.

Total freedom to enter the presence of God with boldness was, as we understand the Scriptures, something with which the Old Testament saints were only faintly acquainted. The God of Israel was the holy, powerful and awesome Sovereign who appeared on Sinai and thundered forth the 'tables of stone'. God was pleased to emphasize, as it were, to the believers of pre-New Testament days his majesty and transcendent glory. The God the pious Israelite knew was the One who rules in the whirlwind and the storm, treads upon the clouds like dust and rebukes the sea, making it dry. The mountains quake before him, the hills melt, and the earth trembles at his presence (Nahum 1:3-5). The Christian serves the same God and bows with the same reverence as the Old Testament believer. But now that Jesus has come and torn away the veil which separated sinners from God's holy presence (Matt. 27:51), there is a new emphasis on peace between God and his people. The sin debt has been fully paid, in actual historical fact, and there is no barrier for the saint who comes through the blood of Jesus.

Yes, without a doubt, the privilege the Christian has of immediate, full, uninhibited access into the presence of God through the priesthood of his Saviour is an inestimable blessing. Just as a loving earthly father cherishes the fellowship with his children and lends a sympathetic ear to all their pleas, even the most trivial, so God the Father welcomes his children to come to him with all their concerns. Truly 'The eyes of the Lord are on the righteous, and his ears are open to their prayers' (1 Peter 3:12). The gate of heaven is open to all God's redeemed family. No, the truth is that there is no gate. The Christian lives in the home of his Father. He is an insider now. He witnesses every day his Father's smile and hears his tender voice.

Yet how little believers seem really to enjoy the inestimable privilege of fellowship with their heavenly Father! How slow they are to claim their rightful place in his heart! How they neglect, to their own hurt, to run to him with faith and assurance, and draw from his paternal care. Instead of coming boldly and confidently, they come hesitating, doubting, fearing, cringing. They are much more prone to turn to feeble, fallible friends or other Christians who usually can administer very little solace and comfort. Even worse, they sink into worry and despondency, unable or unwilling to take their stand on the infallible promises of the Word of God.

> Oh, what peace we often forfeit,
> Oh what needless pain we bear,
> All because we do not carry
> Everything to God in prayer!

Let those of us who have the testimony in our hearts that we are the sons of God learn to claim our birthright more. Our gracious heavenly Father has done everything possible to show us he loves us. He gave the most precious treasure of his heart, his own beloved Son, to die on a cruel cross for our sins. He has entered our lives by his sovereign grace, causing us to seek him. He has given us his Spirit to guide, teach, protect and encourage us. He has provided us his inspired Word to nourish our spirits and counsel us in all the many changing scenes of this world. All we need to do is to believe and trust. All we need to do is to come to him and he will welcome us with open arms. He is waiting to be gracious. He invites us into his presence. He wants us to call him Father, and know truly what that title means in our lives.

4.
Praise: the key element of worship

'Our Father in heaven, Hallowed be your name' (Luke 11:2).

The Lord's instructions to his disciples on the subject of prayer can be broken down into three broad categories. First he gave a *model*, sometimes referred to as 'The Lord's Prayer', for the disciples to use as a guide. Second, he gave a parable, roughly equivalent to what we would call *an illustration*, which focuses on the importance of perseverance in prayer. Third, he gave some amazing, encouraging *promises* which, when when we claim them, can lead to victory in prayer.

No inconsistency between the two versions

We are now ready to begin to examine in detail the *model* Jesus gives his people for praying. Actually there are two versions of this prayer, one recorded in Matthew 6:9-13 and the one we are now considering in Luke 11:2-4. The ideas in them are the same, although the phraseology varies. Liberals jump on the differences in these two versions and allege that this is evidence of 'contradiction' in the teachings of the various Gospels. On the contrary, the differences between the two demonstrate the wisdom of Jesus Christ in his method of teaching the disciples and provide important lessons on the doctrine of the inspiration of the Scriptures.

Obviously Luke's shorter version of the model prayer was given on a later occasion than Matthew's. This shows how patient our Saviour was with his disciples as he sought to teach and lead them into a closer walk with God. Apparently they had not learned the lesson he had given them earlier, so he repeated it for emphasis. Furthermore, the variations between the versions remind us that 'carbon copies' were not the method chosen by the Holy Spirit in supervising the writing of Scripture. The Bible was written before typewriters, computers, or fax machines. There is clear doctrinal and spiritual unity in Scripture, from beginning to end. This unity is in the concepts that are taught, but not in the precise language employed. As the Holy Spirit helped Matthew, Mark, Luke and John to record the teachings of Christ, he led them to emphasize different statements even from the same message, or different details in the same incident, to stress a particular point. For example, Matthew notes that there were two blind men who were healed outside Jericho just before Jesus' triumphal entry. Mark and Luke, however, centre their attention on the more prominent of these two, Bartimæus. Obviously he was more aggressive and stepped forth first for healing. But there is no inconsistency. It is the same situation described from two different perspectives.

In the case of the model prayer, we have recorded in Matthew and Luke the same basic prayer presented by Jesus on different occasions. The two versions are similar enough in style to embody the basic devotional principles Jesus wishes to teach, but different enough in phraseology to show that precise wording in prayer is not important with God.

The model prayer is not a ritual

Could it also be that God in his infinite foresight knew that many people would pervert the model prayer from an example to be studied for its structure and content into a written prayer to be recited mechanically? While the recitation of the model prayer may be understandable and tolerable for a new Christian, I am sure that if it becomes a crutch it ceases to serve the intention for which it was originally given. After all, we can understand that an injured person may wish to use a crutch, but if his condition improves we expect the crutch to be thrown away. Perhaps the Lord has given us two different versions in order to discourage the tendency to turn the model prayer into a thoughtless, mechanical recitation. Have you ever heard people debating about which version to use in a worship service? We do not need to trouble ourselves about which phraseology we should recite in church — 'forgive us our trespasses' or 'forgive us our debts'. It really doesn't matter. The point is that we should incorporate confession into our praying.

Another point needs to be made in opposition to recitation of the Lord's prayer by rote. Most people, no matter how unskilled in language, know how to get their point across to other people, particularly when they are asking for a favour. A poor housewife, a mere simpleton in formal education, knows how to ask her husband for some money for her children. It would be strange to see such a person sitting down to try to compose a precise and formal request and then *read* it to him. Most people know how to explain their symptoms to a doctor spontaneously without writing them down beforehand. Just so, our heavenly Father does not expect us to use formal, written, expertly composed prayers when addressing him. It seems peculiar when God's children cannot tell their Father what is bothering them. Not even the model prayer itself should be used as a substitute for a sincere, earnest, spontaneous plea to our Father. He wants us to come to him and pray with the simple pleas of our hearts, however fumbling and ungrammatical they may be. God is interested in the spirit and intention of prayer, not in a precise form of words.

Nevertheless the model prayer of Jesus provides for us certain crucial elements in true prayer. It is a marvellous prayer, designed by the Lord Jesus himself. It tells us a lot about how to pray. Let us consider some characteristics of this prayer that he uses in responding to the earnest request, 'Lord teach us to pray.'

Characteristics of the model prayer

First, this prayer is *short*. Obviously there are times when the Christian may be led to spend a great deal of time in prayer. A prayer that is inspired by the Holy Spirit could last for hours. But prayer does not need to be long to be meaningful and effective. Sometimes long, drawn-out prayers can reflect a very confused perception of the purpose of praying. Prayers can be lengthened intentionally because of the mistaken opinion that it takes a long time to get God's attention. Jesus warned in the Sermon on the Mount that we should avoid prayers that are long because of 'vain repetitions': 'But when you pray, do not use vain repetitions as the heathen do. For they think that they will be heard for their many words. Therefore do not be like them. For your Father knows the things you have need of before you ask him' (Matt. 6:7-8). It was immediately after this that he told them to pray 'in this manner' — and then gave them the model prayer.

When Jesus speaks of 'vain repetitions' he is definitely condemning the incantations of the pagan worshippers. They mouthed, then as now, meaningless expressions over and over again, often accompanied with violent gyrations and contortions of body. (An example of silly repetitions are the 'mantras' which are a part of the Transcendental Meditation exercise.) Such exhibitions often reflect a doubt about the willingness of the deity to hear, or even about the reality of the power behind it.

Jesus could also be cautioning his own children against the view that the effectiveness of prayer is based on its duration. We should not entertain the suspicion that God is reluctant to hear and answer, or that lengthy prayers are essential to induce him to be favourable to us. Short prayers, if uttered in sincerity and trust, are as pleasing to God as lengthy ones.

Second, the model prayer is *simple*. Prayer-making has become a sort of art form in some Christian circles. One often goes to public occasions, even church services, and hears prayers which were obviously composed with literary value in mind. They droll on and on, with smooth and florid expressions that are really void of meaning. Such prayers are often collected, printed and circulated, with the hopes that the linguistic skills of their authors will be admired. The whole thing, frankly, is an abomination. The prayer that Jesus gave his disciples embodies profound concepts, to be sure, but they are given in simple words that even a child can understand. There is nothing mysterious, esoteric (pardon the big word in condemning big words!), or pompous about the model prayer. Jesus wants the prayers of his people to be like this. The simple, sincere cry of a soul longing to talk to God is heard, while the elaborate and florid compositions of many preachers, designed to sound impressive, are worthless in God's sight. It was just such public displays of piety which were performed by the Pharisees and were denounced by Jesus (see Matt. 6:5).

Third, the model prayer is *balanced*. All the basic elements in prayer — praise, thanksgiving, confession and petition — are contained either explicitly or implicitly in this prayer. It is remarkably compact, terse and comprehensive. There is nothing superfluous or trite here. In a brief scope we are given all the essential dimensions of prayer.

The primary place of praise and adoration

We need to take note of the *order* of our supplications to the Father, as outlined in the model prayer given by Jesus. He is clearly, unquestionably, prescribing that all prayer should begin by the worship of the Father. All other aspects of prayer, based on the Saviour's model, such as confession, intercession and petition, logically are to come after adoration. How appropriate this is! No Christian service or devotion can be acceptable to God except that which starts with the supreme motive of honouring and glorifying the name of the great Sovereign who has saved us. 'Lord supply our needs,' 'Lord forgive us our sins,' 'Lord, pour out your blessings on our church,' are all worthy prayers that should be uttered. But, fitting and important as they are, they should, in the order of things, come after God has been properly praised.

The first words of the model prayer are words which ascribe glory and honour to God: 'Hallowed be your name.' The word for 'hallowed' in this passage (precisely the same Greek word and form is found in Matthew 6:9) is used twenty-eight times in the New Testament and literally means 'sanctified'. It is translated 'sanctified' in every instance except in Revelation 22:11, where we read, 'Let him be *holy* still,' and in the two versions of the model prayer, where 'hallowed' is used. The English word 'hallow' is roughly equivalent to 'sanctify' and means to consecrate for a holy or sacred use. This word has been so established in the traditional model prayer as originally contained in the Authorized Version that it is retained in almost all modern translations, including the New International Version. The Berkeley Version says, 'Thy name be held holy'; the Living Bible paraphrases: 'May your name be honoured for its holiness.'

If we view this invocation, 'Hallowed be your name,' in the light of the Old Testament Scriptures, we should have no doubt as to its meaning. The name of God in the language of the Bible stands for God's person — all that he is. God's name means his perfections, his attributes, his glory. To sanctify the name of God means to ascribe supreme honour to him and to worship him with reverence and trust. Consider the following Old Testament texts: 'Blessed be your glorious name, which is exalted above all blessing and praise!' (Neh. 9:5); 'O Lord, our Lord, how excellent is your name in all the earth' (Ps. 8:1); 'Revive us, and we will call upon your name' (Ps. 80:18).

We all regard our names as symbolic of our persons. When we sign our names, or read them in print, we see ourselves identified. God has many names in Scripture. In addition to the general term for God, there is the Old Testament covenant name of God, Yahweh. The name of God is to be hallowed because it speaks of the great and glorious One who created us, redeemed us and keeps us. We hallow, sanctify, or consecrate the name of God when we worship him, adore him and praise him. Also we hallow his name when we use it with reverence. As Robert Murray M'Cheyne said, 'The highest act of Christian service is worship.'

How important it is that in our public worship services the element of praise is kept in prominence! Scriptures that ascribe glory and praise to God should be read. Hymns that lead the church in exalted worship should be selected. Themes that draw out the gratitude and praise of the saints, such as the love and mercy of God, the atonement of Jesus and God's invitation to sinners, should be the main topics of the pulpit. The people should be encouraged to come to the services with the spirit of gratitude and praise. They should be there to sanctify the name of God, not to find something to criticize, or to air their complaints to other brothers and sisters.

Like most evangelical churches our own has a Wednesday evening prayer meeting. The format remained the same for many years. There was some singing, a Bible study and then 'prayer time'. People always had a long list of things to 'pray about'. Often people who cannot find time to attend the meeting pass on requests for prayer, usually about something physical.

There is nothing wrong with this, and we always are glad to pray for people. But it occurred to me one day that the prayer meetings in our church were too much like Old MacDonald's wife: 'Gimme gimme here, gimme gimme there, here gimme, there gimme, everywhere gimme, gimme.' In other words, all we were doing at prayer meetings was taking our shopping list to the Lord. Then I read Psalm 33:1, which says, 'Praise from the upright is beautiful.' I realized that we were not really praising the Lord in the prayer meeting. I decided at that point that the participation part of prayer meeting would *begin* with matters of praise and thanksgiving to God. No one is to make a request, or voice a need, until there has been an opportunity for people to share a Scripture which has been a blessing, or give a word of thanks to God for some mercy. Although the transition from the shopping list concept to the praise concept has been difficult and slow, it is catching on. A new spirit is breathing in our prayer meeting. It is even, after many years of stagnation, beginning to grow numerically.

We should practise the same principle in our private devotions. All of us have had the experience of going to God and finding our hearts cold as ice. Frankly, at times, we do not really want to pray. We are on our knees out of sheer devotion to our duty. It's prayer time, and now we are about to pray, but the spirit of prayer is not there. What should we do?

I have found that when I am in this condition it helps a lot to begin to think about the great God to whom we are praying. If your mind is spiritually frigid or distracted, just be quiet and reflect on the attributes of God. Consider his power and wisdom. Think about his universal presence throughout the universe. Think about his self-sufficiency and his eternity. Think about his love and grace in providing for our salvation. I find that after a few moments of meditation like this the Spirit of God begins to blow over the dying coals of devotion in my heart. I feel some glow in my soul and soon, as a rule, the flame of love is burning. The point is that thinking about who God is and what he has done inspires true prayer.

Prayer should begin and end with God. As Jonathan Edwards stressed over and over again, God delights in himself and is committed to his own glory. If we are in tune with his sovereign purposes we will also set his glory as our supreme desire. When we pray we should want to hallow or sanctify his name. This is where the Lord himself taught us to start.

5.
Priority: the kingdom of God

'Your kingdom come. Your will be done on earth as it is in heaven'
(Luke 11:2).

'Power to the people.'

This powerful slogan is catching on all over the world as modern man's longing for freedom and democracy bursts forth. Old tyrannies are breaking up, oppressive political systems are crumbling and new forms of government which recognize the rights of the individual are taking their place. Although such movements can end in anarchy and chaos if respect for law is not recognized, we must all applaud these developments and take advantage of them for the gospel.

Unfortunately, egalitarian concepts are often transferred into the realm of God's government. Some people assume that because democracy works best in human politics, therefore God's kingdom is a democracy. Many modern Christians seem to think that man's freedom, decisions, interests and rights are at the top of the list of priorities in theology. One almost gets the impression, in listening to some religious teachers, that God himself holds authority by the suffrage of humanity. Someone even caricatured this theology as teaching that God was 'up for vote'. In this surrealistic world the 'free will of man' is exalted and the 'free will of God' is ridiculed.

Those who are influenced by this essentially humanistic philosophy must inevitably be shocked, perhaps even deeply offended, when they read the Bible and discover the real situation. They find that while man is held accountable for his moral condition, the truth is that it is God, not man, who reigns. God's sovereign dominion comes by virtue of his essential and inherent power and glory, not by the vote or approval of any creature. 'He sits on no precarious throne, nor borrows leave to be.'

God's sovereignty is reflected in the nature of the new order introduced by his Son Jesus Christ. The Bible teaches that Jesus Christ came to introduce a kingdom, not a constitutional republic, much less a pure democracy. The section of the model prayer now under consideration, 'Your kingdom come,' reminds us that in dealing with God we are dealing with supreme, eternal, indisputable *sovereignty*. In fact, Jesus taught that the very essence of piety is to become interested in the triumph of the kingdom of God.

There is a close connection between the adoration of God and the prayer that his kingdom will prevail on earth. 'Hallowed be your name' focuses on the *essential* glory and majesty of God. After all, God should be worshipped for who he is, apart from any consideration of his works, such as creation or redemption. Obviously God existed prior to any of his works. He reigned in supreme splendour and happiness before the universe, the angels, or mankind existed. He would have continued to be glorious had he never chosen to create anyone to appreciate or love him. On the other hand, 'Your kingdom come,' draws our attention to God's *manifested* glory, that is, God s greatness and power as seen in what he actually does in time and space. We need to praise God for what he has done.

Several questions come before us as we consider the petition, 'Your kingdom come.' First, what is this kingdom that Jesus is talking about? Exactly how is this kingdom to 'come'? The subject of the kingdom of God is a fascinating and important study. It bears materially on many other biblical doctrines and themes.

What is the kingdom?

The concept of the kingdom of God originated in the Old Testament period. The God of the Hebrews was acknowledged as a King; in fact before the monarchy was established in the days of the prophet Samuel he was the only king Israel had. Jeremiah confessed the faith of the devout Hebrew when he said, 'But the Lord is the true God; he is the living God and the everlasting King' (10:10). Even though Israel had earthly kings who ruled over them, these regimes were only dim reflections of the sovereign rule of Yahweh; in fact they derived their validity only from his permission. King David, as he was about to transfer power to his son Solomon and pass into eternity, yielded his sceptre, as it were, with deference to the true

King whom he served. Before all the congregation he prayed,

> 'Yours, O Lord, is the greatness,
> The power and the glory,
> The victory and the majesty;
> For all that is in heaven and in earth is yours;
> Yours is the kingdom, O Lord,
> And you are exalted as head over all'
>
> (1 Chron. 29:11).

It is plain beyond question that when Jesus Christ entered his public ministry a new phase of the kingdom of God was being initiated. Early in his ministry we are told that Jesus preached 'the gospel of the kingdom of God' (Mark 1:14). 'The time is fulfilled,' he said, 'and the kingdom of God is at hand. Repent, and believe in the gospel' (v.15). During his early itinerary among the villages which ringed the Sea of Galilee, he cried out, 'Repent, for the kingdom of heaven is at hand' (Matt. 4:17), using the same words which John the Baptist had used as he sought to prepare his hearers for the ministry of Jesus (Matt. 3:1).[1]

If God was acknowledged as the Sovereign of heaven and earth in the Old Testament period, then in what sense was the kingdom suddenly 'at hand' when Jesus appeared on the scene? On the surface there is something strange, almost ludicrous, about the audacious message of John and Jesus: 'Get ready, the kingdom is here!' Here was a leather-clad denizen of the desert, dining on nothing but locusts and honey, speaking of a 'kingdom'. Here was a humble carpenter from the despised little town of Nazareth boldly echoing that same theme to the people of Palestine. What kind of kingdom is this?

The answer is not hard to come by. The truth is that the son of Joseph and Mary, who had grown up at Nazareth under the tutelage of the local elders of the synagogue and followed the carpentry trade of his father, was himself the King. Although his royal glory was veiled and obscured by his human nature, and though his kingdom was different in kind from what one might have first anticipated, Jesus was none other than the promised King of Israel. It was announced at his birth that as the occupant of the throne of his father David he would reign over the house of Jacob for ever and have an everlasting kingdom (Luke 1:32-33). How was the kingdom 'at hand' in this period of history? Simply put, the kingdom was at hand because the King was at hand, and he was about to select his first subjects. When the King comes, the kingdom comes.

It is easy to see from the teachings of Jesus that the kingdom of God was uppermost in his mind. The very words by which John the Baptist introduced him were formulated in terms of the kingdom: 'Repent, for the kingdom ... is at hand.' Jesus taught that faith, discipleship and service to God are all kingdom experiences. The 'new birth' incorporates people into the 'kingdom of God' (John 3:5). The self-denying spirit of a person who is setting aside material concerns for the pursuit of eternal values is by definition 'seeking first the kingdom of God' (Matt. 6:33). When a person is seriously enquiring about the way of following God and listening carefully to the claims of the King, he is 'not far from the kingdom of God' (Mark 12:34). Most of Jesus' parables sought to illustrate what the kingdom of God is 'like'. They explain the 'mysteries of the kingdom of heaven' (Matt. 13:11).

Jesus explicitly claimed, in fact, to be a king. Although he firmly resisted an early attempt to install him as sovereign over some ill-conceived, carnal concept of local rule (John 6:15), he acknowledged royal prerogatives. When Pontius Pilate asked Jesus if he were a king, Jesus' reply was: 'You say rightly that I am a king' (John 18:37). Of course he made it quite clear that the dominion over which he ruled was not (at this time at least) visible and physical but spiritual. 'My kingdom is not of this world,' he affirmed (John 18:36).

Jesus claimed to be invested with sovereign authority to administer in the name of his Father who sent him. In fact Jesus demanded for himself the same honour and worship to which the Father himself was entitled: 'For the Father judges no one, but has committed all judgement to the Son, that all should honour the Son just as they honour the Father' (John 5:22-23). He claimed to have authority over all flesh that he should give eternal life to those given to him by the Father (John 17:2). Jesus revealed that this authority was limitless in extent, embracing the whole universe in its scope: 'All authority has been given to me in heaven and on earth' (Matt. 28:18).

Soon after Jesus' public ministry was inaugurated, he began to back up his awesome claims with works which lay beyond the power of any mere mortal. He demonstrated his sovereign power by conquering disease (Mark 1:34), multiplying food (John 6:11-13), ridding many of demonic possession (Matt. 12:27) and suspending the laws of nature (Mark 6:48). Interestingly, Jesus stated specifically that his exorcisms brought to earth the kingdom of God (Matt. 12:28). Truly, for those who had eyes to see, for those who were not hopelessly blinded by their own prejudices and subject to satanic delusion, Jesus verified his claim to sovereign power. Although he was poor, despised and falsely accused, indisputable evidences that he was indeed the King of glory flashed forth from his person.

The authenticity of Jesus' claim to sovereign power was not limited to his miraculous works on earth. The Gospel record affirms that although he was eventually put to death by crucifixion, he rose again from the dead and spent several weeks with his disciples. In the book of Acts we are told that he ascended into heaven (Acts 1:9-11). We learn also that upon his ascension to heaven he was exalted to the right hand of God and enthroned officially as Lord of heaven and earth (Acts 2:30-36). Peter, who preached the first great sermon after Jesus' departure to heaven, announced to the people of Jerusalem that Jesus reigned in sovereign majesty, carrying out a plan which would eventually terminate in the destruction of all his enemies (Acts 2:35).

In summary, the kingdom of God is simply God's rule over men and nations through the mediatorial sovereignty of his Son, Jesus Christ. The plan unveiled in Scripture is not that the triune God in his essential glory rules over the universe, but that the Second Person, Jesus Christ, has been appointed as Lord over all creation. The New Testament makes it clear that the kingdom which was *introduced* by the early preaching of John the Baptist, and *explained* by the teachings of Christ himself, was officially *established* when he ascended to reign at the right hand of the Father. We can see from this that Jesus Christ is not now a refugee on the throne of heaven, as some have claimed, but the 'King of kings and Lord of lords' (1 Tim. 6:15).

When will the kingdom come?

If, as I trust has been shown, the kingdom of God is now a present reality, as present as the session of Jesus at the Father's right hand, how can we expect this kingdom to 'come' at some future time? This question must be answered if we are to interpret the petition which forms a part of the model prayer.

Christians are generally agreed on the answer to this question, although there is some difference of interpretation on details. They agree that when the doctrines, commandments and interests of their Saviour are adhered to, God's kingdom is advanced. They agree that when souls, under the dominion of Satan, are delivered from sin and yield in loving submission to Christ as Lord, the kingdom comes. They agree that when Christians, through the instructions of faithful leaders in the church, grow in grace and knowledge, God's kingdom advances. They agree that when God's visible church on earth comes closer and closer to the standard of conduct set in the example of Christ and the teachings of the apostles, the interests of God's kingdom are enhanced.

The kingdom of God in its present form, considered as a historical reality, has already made great progress. The followers of Christ were in the beginning a very small band, just over 100. They were a despised, persecuted sect, essentially void of any real power or influence. But that has changed dramatically. In our modern world Jesus Christ numbers among those who profess to follow him a considerable segment of the world's population. Although many are no doubt only nominal followers, and although many who wear the name Christian shamefully disgrace his cause by the way they live, still the church of Christ is indisputably a powerful force in the world. Throughout the nearly twenty centuries since Jesus returned to heaven the church has preached his gospel. Scarcely a nation in history, certainly none which is civilized, has been untouched by the power of the gospel of Christ.

But is this all? Is there not some fuller, more visible development of the kingdom of God? Assessing in the most optimistic terms the impact of Christianity in modern society, we must say, in all candour, that the world still, like in the days of John the apostle, 'lies under the sway of the wicked one' (1 John 5:19). In general, those in high positions of authority have never had much regard for the claims of Jesus Christ. Human governments have, for the most part, been motivated by greed and lust for dominance. The masses of people living on planet Earth, generally speaking, live in blatant disregard of the dictates and standards of Holy Scripture. This is true both in regard to the highly civilized and industrialized nations of the Western world, and the still largely backward 'undeveloped' communities of the 'Third World'.

The situation within what is supposed to be the household of God itself is not totally encouraging. The church of Christ, which was ordained by its sovereign Head to be salt to preserve the earth and light to penetrate and dispel its intellectual darkness, is awfully compromised and ineffective. Prominent leaders in some sections of the 'visible church', even those established on sound theological principles, undermine the kingdom of God by teaching damnable heresies. Far too many who name the name of Christ, though members of the church and occasionally attentive to the forms of worship, live in open sin. Surely, if this is the coming of the kingdom of God for which the church is to pray, it certainly has not risen to the level of hope that the original promise seemed to encourage.

Christians believe that there is a future and final aspect of the kingdom of God. They believe that Jesus Christ is going to come again and settle once and for all the whole issue of man's rebellion against the Creator. They believe that the dead, both the righteous and the wicked, will be raised and assigned to their appropriate eternal reward. They believe this because Jesus himself so taught (John 5:28-29). They believe that God will some day hold court, in the person of his Son Jesus, and that all men and nations will be judged. They base this on Jesus' own teachings (Matt. 25:31-46). They believe that the children of God will be ushered into an eternal home of happiness and glory, while the enemies of Christ will suffer the unspeakable fate of eternal separation from God. This, too, was clearly taught by Christ himself (see John 14:2-3; Mark 9:42-50; Matt. 25:31-46). They believe that the present heavens and earth will be destroyed and there will be a new order, free from sin and pain. This is implied in the teachings of Jesus and plainly outlined in the writings of his apostles (Matt. 13:41-43; 2 Peter 3:10-13; Rev. 21:1-4).

It deserves to be said, however, in all fairness, that the majority of Christians have held that there will be some intermediate manifestation of the kingdom of God between its present state of limited influence and the ultimate final consummation. A 'latter day glory' hope has filled the vision of many great Christian teachers. Some, such as Jonathan Edwards, Andrew Fuller, Augustus Hopkins Strong and Benjamin Warfield, have believed that this glorious day will precede the final, literal second coming of Christ. Others, such as many of the early Church Fathers, John Gill, John Charles Ryle and Andrew Bonar, were convinced that this period would follow the second coming of Christ. But all agree that Jesus is now reigning over a spiritual kingdom and that his sovereignty will eventually prevail over the whole earth and will be acknowledged by the subjugation of every influence contrary to him.

Praying for the coming of the kingdom

Praying for the kingdom of our Lord to come includes, as I understand it, petition for both phases of the kingdom — the present and the future. Let us consider for a moment the implications of praying for the prosperity of the *present* aspect of the kingdom.

If the kingdom of Jesus Christ is advanced when sinners are converted, then without question the people of God should sincerely, frequently, pray for *evangelistic efforts*. It is interesting to note that Jesus' last command to the church before ascending into heaven was the command to evangelize. In the so-called Great Commission of Matthew 28:16-20 Jesus reminds the disciples that to him has been committed all authority in heaven and in earth. With this foundation laid he now says, 'Go therefore and make disciples of all the nations, baptizing them in the name of the Father and of the Son and of the Holy Spirit, teaching them to observe all things that I have commanded you; and lo, I am with you always, even to the end of the age' (vv. 19-20). This passage shows that evangelism is based on the sovereignty and lordship of Christ. Since this is so, evangelism is kingdom work. When the church takes the gospel into a world which lies in spiritual ignorance and is bound by the chains of sin, it is invading, as it were, the kingdom of darkness. Every time a soul is truly converted Satan's dominion is diminished.

It is very important to realize that the work of evangelism and missions must be undertaken with trust in God and prayer. It is a work that simply cannot be done by human strength. The church may have all the physical assets to preach the gospel to the lost. It may have a beautiful building, talented preachers and modern technological devices to spread the gospel, but it is all in vain unless God is pleased to bless the church's efforts. How we can praise God for the tools that the scientific age has brought us: printing presses, the radio, television, satellites, cassette recorders, copying machines and the computer! But it is the Word of God which the Lord blesses in the salvation of souls. All the devices just mentioned can be used just as effectively to spread error or corrupt the human mind.

They can also be used, of course, to lead and teach men in the ways of God.

When Jesus Christ sent out the early disciples, seventy in number, to minister the gospel, he sought to impress upon them the tremendous needs of their fellow men. He pictured to them the world as a vast harvest field with the grain begging to be reaped. 'The harvest truly is great,' he said (Luke 10:2). Even those of us who are farthest removed from the agricultural setting in which this statement was made can appreciate the force of Jesus' words. He obviously is comparing the masses of humanity without the gospel to a large field of ripe grain waiting to be harvested. By comparing the lost sinners of the world to a harvest field Jesus is not only pointing out mankind's spiritual needs, but also he is emphasizing the urgency of the moment. When the harvest is ready there can be no delay. The crop must either be reaped or it will perish. Such, Jesus says, is the situation in an unconverted world. Every generation, every community has its harvest of souls. There should be no delay in the attempt to preach the gospel to them.

However, what is more relevant to our present subject, it is very interesting to note the specific measure Jesus recommends in accepting the great challenge of reaping souls. He demands of the disciples prayer as the first duty, coming before even the work of evangelization itself: 'Pray the Lord of the harvest to send out labourers into his harvest' (Luke 10:2). He is seeking to remind the disciples that God's providence and guidance must undergird true evangelism. When it gets the vision of world missions and evangelism the church is first to *pray*. Pray for what? Pray that God himself will raise up true ministers, evangelists and missionaries to reap the harvest. Gathering in souls must be done by true servants of God if it is to be done effectively. Evangelistic effort, no matter how energetic, that is not done by people who have been commissioned by God himself will not accomplish what God intends. Imagine a clumsy, unskilled, amateur, unfamiliar with the gathering of grain, thrashing about in a field with his scythe. Such a person would do more harm than good. Just so, evangelism needs people who really understand the needs of men and have a thorough grasp of gospel truths if it is to be effective.

Needless to say, the church should not only pray for God to call labourers to fill the harvest field, but it should pray for the power of the Holy Spirit to attend the teaching of the gospel. Just as the early disciples had to tarry for the coming of the Spirit, we need to seek divine anointing in our work of evangelism. Let us never forget that it is not by might nor by power that success attends the preaching of the Word, but by God's Spirit (Zech. 4:6).

Yet, in spite of the clear admonition of Jesus, Christian people often undertake evangelism without the proper dependence upon God, either for an understanding of the correct biblical methods of evangelism, or the absolute need for the power of the Spirit to make it effective. Certainly God blesses his truth, no matter how imperfectly delivered, or no matter how misguided are some of its bearers. But much more good is done when the church is humbly seeking God's leadership, God's power and God's blessing on its efforts to win the lost.

Not only should believers seek God's help in evangelism and missions, but all phases of Christian enterprise should, to use an expression that has perhaps been overworked, be 'bathed in prayer'. Such efforts as teaching in Sunday School, book publication and distribution, Christian colleges and seminaries, as well as the ministries of the local churches, suffer from lack of prayer commitment on the part of God's people. Because of prayerlessness false doctrines creep into the churches. Because of prayerlessness needless divisions and disputes disrupt progress in Christian ministry. Because of prayerlessness pastors, teachers and evangelists return from their toils discouraged and defeated. In short, the kingdom of Jesus Christ prospers and thrives only when those who support it rely on God and demonstrate that reliance by faithful prayer.

In conclusion, just a word about prayer for *the final manifestation* of the kingdom of God. This is admittedly a difficult subject and receives, not surprisingly, little attention among those who believe in the sovereignty of God's purposes. God has promised that his Son will some day return to earth and will bring about the final solution to the long history of Satan's rebellion and man's apostasy. There is no doubt about it. The dead will some day be raised, all men will be judged, and the two classes of people, saved and unsaved, will be assigned to their eternal habitations. If this is certain to happen, should we pray for its fulfilment?

I believe that Christians should pray for Jesus' return even though in God's plan it is an absolute certainty. The Bible ends on the prayer of John, the author of Revelation: 'Even so, come Lord

Jesus' (Rev. 22:20). Peter says that the church is 'looking for and hastening the coming of the day of God' (2 Peter 3:12). 'Hastening' seems to mean looking forward to with earnest expectation. What true believer, when he feels the heavy weight of sin upon his own conscience and witnesses the continual assault upon God's glory all about him, does not naturally cry out to God for the final intervention that will put down Satan's kingdom? How man's prayers fit into the purpose of God for his final intervention is a matter upon which we cannot speculate. One thing is clear: the God who decrees an event in time not infrequently accomplishes that event through human means and instrumentality. Prayer is the means God uses to carry out his plans.

What a glorious day it will be when God's will is done on this earth as it now is 'in heaven'! In heaven all is order and perfect harmony. The angels bow in adoring submission to the King of kings and Lord of lords. They do his bidding without question or hesitation. Some day it will be that way on earth. Every force, every thought that is antagonistic to the perfect will of God in Christ will be put down. Satan and all his hosts will be cast into the regions of eternal darkness. The earth, once cursed with sin and now groaning like a woman in birth pangs (Rom. 8:22), will eventually be the scene of uninterrupted righteousness and peace. Then 'The kingdoms of this world have become the kingdoms of our Lord and of his Christ, and he shall reign for ever and ever!' (Rev. 11:15). The vast host of the redeemed, a great multitude that no man can number, will live for ever in intimate fellowship with their God. Let us pray for this to come soon: 'Your kingdom come. Your will be done on earth as it is in heaven.'

1. Heaven is the throne of God and thus is used by synectoche to refer to God himself. The kingdom of God is the same as the kingdom of heaven.

6.
Petition: prayer for personal needs

'Give us day by day our daily bread' (Luke 11:2).

By incorporating this simple petition in the model prayer Jesus descends, as it were, from the lofty heights of the worship of God and longing for the triumph of his kingdom, to the lowlands of man's own personal concerns. God knows that his children are a needy people and he expects them to pray about those needs. We are not only spiritual beings, but also physical and emotional beings as well. To be sure, human happiness depends on a proper relationship with God. Worshipping and serving God should have a pre-eminent place in our daily routine. The model prayer acknowledges the spiritual dimension of life. But life is more than going to church, praying and reading the Bible. The Creator has placed us in this world. To survive in it we need food, clothing and shelter. We need jobs, families and stable government to have a meaningful existence.

Self-denial is certainly an integral part of being a Christian. Indeed Jesus plainly taught that one who makes selfish interests the chief and dominating motive of life cannot be counted among his disciples (Matt. 10:34-39). But self-denial is not the same as self-repudiation or self-negation. The will to survive and succeed in life is a gift of God to us by creation. Self-interest is not wrong.

God's concern for his people's welfare

I would like to make a confession at this point. Early in my Christian life, through a distorted emphasis of some respected teachers, and through a misinterpretation of some passages of Scripture, I developed a view that God had a kind of ambivalent plan for his people. I had come to believe that one phase had to do with what God intends for his children in this life and one pertained to his designs for them in the next life. In short, almost without even being aware of the heresy, I had adopted the view that God wanted his people to be miserable this side of the grave and happy in heaven. Out of this grew a sort of guilt complex about personal happiness and prosperity. I now see that this was all a great mistake.

Jesus taught that God is looking out for the welfare of his children in every aspect of their sojourn here on earth. Certainly he has not promised, absolutely, that they will always be 'healthy and wealthy'. Certainly he has not given to any one of them a guarantee that they will be free from the ordinary afflictions of life, such as poverty, bereavement, loneliness, or death. On the contrary, not only are believers subject to the same problems as the world, but there are special difficulties that are part and parcel of following Jesus Christ. 'In the world,' Jesus once said to the disciples, 'you will have tribulation' (John 16:33). They were warned that the world would hate them just as it hated him (John 15:18).

Yes, because of the sin that entered the world through Adam, the followers of Christ often experience pain and suffering. But all God's works for believers are redemptive. Affliction is incidental to God's plan for his own. 'He does not afflict willingly, nor grieve the children of men' (Lam. 3:33). Suffering is never represented in Scripture as an end in itself, but as a means to spiritual growth and development. Even when God chastens his people for their waywardness, he does it for their own good, not simply to administer discomfort.

Although sickness is the actual situation of many of his children, health and wholeness is God's ultimate plan. But health is many-faceted. The human personality is a complex combination of physical, mental and emotional functions. Our physical, emotional and spiritual welfare are all related. Physical disease can produce mental distress and even spiritual declension. Mental distress can lead to physical pain and backsliding. And what true Christian can really enjoy a healthy body or mind if his spirit is sorely tried by a raging battle with sin and temptation?

The disciples to whom Jesus ministered when he lived here on earth were essentially no different from God's people in any age, including ourselves. They were sometimes sceptical, fearful and discouraged. They needed to be taught how to trust in God instead of worrying. They needed the strong hand of Jesus their Master to lead them, strengthen them and help them to carry their burdens. Christ's own description of them as 'sheep' is very instructive. Sheep are notoriously helpless, vulnerable and foolish. Yet they are beautiful animals and can easily be loved.

A portion of the Sermon on the Mount, and a marvellous one at that, is devoted by the Saviour to assuring the disciples of their heavenly Father's tender care for them. In it he counsels faith instead of fear, confidence instead of worry, and idealism rather than carnal ambition.

Matthew 6:25-34 is a passage which should be studied in conjunction with the words, 'Give us this day our daily bread,' in the model prayer. The theme is about the basic necessities of life, such as food, drink and clothing. Three times Jesus specifically tells the disciples not to worry about these things (vv. 25, 31, 34). Twice he states that worry is futile (vv. 27, 28).

The all-sufficiency of God

Nowhere in the Bible is God's power, love, tenderness and providential care set forth more clearly than in the Saviour's instruction in Matthew 6:25-34. Images drawn from God's marvellous creation are freely used to encourage the disciples. On numerous occasions Jesus' disciples displayed crippling fear in the face of this or that danger. Perhaps he had just seen some exhibition of that fretfulness and anxiety that we find so common to human nature just before he gave these lessons in faith. His admonition, 'Do not worry about your life, what you will eat or what you will drink; nor about your body, what you will put on' (v. 25) was almost certainly based on his observation of their present situation. Jesus knew that they were prone to fret about how they could 'make ends meet' and provide for themselves and their own. Perhaps some of them were at this time under some unusual financial pressure.

Notice how the Lord allays their fears. He calls their attention to the birds of the air who, though neither sowing nor reaping, are fed by the heavenly Father. 'Are you not of more value than they?' he asks (v. 26). He even counsels them to learn a lesson from the lilies of the field, which do not toil nor spin, yet are arrayed in a glory greater than that of Solomon (vv. 28-29). Even the very grass of the field, which is destined eventually to be burned, is decked out as in a beautiful garment by the Creator. 'Will he not much more clothe you, O you of little faith?' (v. 30).

Who would have thought of finding encouragement in fowls, flowers and fields? It is doubtful if the woebegone disciples had even considered how nature itself teaches a lesson in faith. Probably they had not taken encouragement in God's providential care of the natural world, or if so the lesson had recently eluded them. Yet the Saviour patiently, gently, urges them to study the natural works of God as a demonstration of his goodness.

Although the lesson in faith which Jesus teaches here is simple, there are powerful theological implications as well. The high concept that Jesus held of God's creative power and providential control of the world is easily lost in thinking about the glory of nature. Unfortunately, some even deny God's providence altogether.

The God that Jesus Christ proclaimed to the despondent disciples was a God who feeds the birds, designs the flowers and adorns the grass in the field with artistic touch. In an age which has, or wishes to have, a scientific explanation for everything, this may seem strange, primitive and naive. Do we believe today that God really is in control of nature? Do we really believe the biblical record that the heavens and earth were designed and made by God? Do we believe that everything, from the fluttering of the feathers on the bird soaring above the earth to the stirring of each particle of dust on the busy street, is directed by God? Jesus believed and taught this. He taught the disciples that no sparrow could fall apart from the heavenly Father's will (Matt. 10:29). He even stated that God knows the exact number of the hairs on our heads (Matt. 10:30). Do we believe this today?

If we do not believe this, then certainly it is useless even to talk about faith in God and prayer. A God who is not in control of the universe might conceivably be a sympathetic and kind being, but if he does not manage all the forces in the world, both natural and spiritual, there is no reason to pray to him. Why ask God to do something he cannot do? Prayer to God, if it is to be something other than an empty ritual, presupposes God's sovereignty, foreknowledge and omnipotence.

When any prayer is answered, even the simplest, the whole machinery of God's government of the world is brought into motion. A single answer to prayer may involve a thousand events, including decisions made by free agents who are totally unaware that God's hand is guiding them. Sometimes even tragedies in our lives can be a tool of God and illustrate the principle that 'All things work together for good to those who love God, to those who are the called according to his purpose' (Rom. 8:28).

Not long ago I was facing a major decision pertaining to a particular area of my own life and ministry. A meeting had been set up to discuss the matter with two brethren who were directly involved in the matter. This was a very important occasion for me. Much time had been spent in prayer. The meeting, which had been scheduled several weeks in advance, was in January. The day turned out to be bitterly cold. As I looked out that morning I debated whether I should go for my usual five-mile run. I decided to go, against my own better judgement (and I might add, against the advice of my wife). Midway in my run I felt a strange sensation in my chest and knew that something was not right. I ended the trek in a slow walk, not in a run. To make a long story short, I ended up in hospital with a mild heart attack. The meeting was cancelled.

Strange though it may seem to many people, I am convinced that God was behind this whole episode. Had this meeting come off as I had planned I probably would have become involved in a course of action which would have sent me in a direction that was not God's will at the time. The two months I spent recuperating from this health problem were a very profitable time of learning for me. There is no doubt that God answered my prayer, but in a way entirely different from what I had expected.

Think for a moment about all the cogs in the wheels of God's providence that interacted in the above scenario. I did not know when this meeting was planned that it would be extremely cold, but God did. I did not know that I would decide to test my lungs and heart with a five-mile run, but God did. God knew about the travel plans that had to change. God knew about the climatological forces which had to develop to cause the near-zero weather pattern. I could easily have decided to stay in and not do my exercise. But sufficient motives were there to propel me out into the streets. Before the whole episode was over medical facilities were engaged. Family life was disrupted. Changes were made in the church schedule. In my opinion, all these details were under the administration of God's providence. My life was redirected because of the whole situation. God intervened.

Special provisions of the prayer

Now that we have surveyed the general import of the prayer, 'Give us day by day our daily bread,' and probed into the theological presuppositions of this petition, it will be profitable to examine more carefully the specifics of this prayer. It is worthy of note that Jesus encourages his disciples to pray for their daily *bread*. Bread is a very common and ordinary food, one of the basics of the human diet. Bread is not something which is necessary for a life of luxury and opulence; it merely sustains life. This is a modest request. There is nothing particularly ambitious or adventuresome in the plea for bread for our table.

Is Jesus Christ subtly reminding his disciples that they are not to make wealth and material prosperity a goal of their lives? On this point some caution is necessary. Nowhere does the Bible condemn prosperity and riches as such. Many of the eminent saints of Scripture were wealthy: Abraham, Solomon, Joseph of Arimathea, to name a few. In God's providential direction, and with his blessing, many of his people are granted a superabundance of earthly goods. Thank God for that, for God uses the prosperity of his children to support Christian enterprise.

Yet Jesus warned his disciples over and over again that there is a great snare in riches. To possess much of this world's goods may be God's design for us, but when material things possess us we are in great peril. The Saviour gave a parable which was specifically designed to serve as a warning to those who strive for wealth, hoard their possessions and are not generous. In Luke 12:13-21 we are told about the sad final state of a man who devoted his life to wealth and pleasure and forgot God. The lesson of the parable was plain: 'And he said to them, "Take heed and beware of covetousness, for one's life does not consist in the abundance of the things he possesses"' (Luke 12:15). Poverty and destitution can certainly be a great trial. They can cause envy and bitterness. But the temptations of riches are a hundredfold worse. Material prosperity and wealth, if not accepted with humility and dependence on God, can lead to pride, carnal security and worldiness.

The modest prayer, 'Give us this day our daily bread,' serves as a curb to the selfish ambitions in all of us. Christ taught his disciples that they should seek *first* the kingdom of God, with the added promise that 'All these things shall be added to you' (Matt. 6:33). There is no harm in the desire to succeed or make a profit as long as we do not lose sight of the real goals of life. Christ and his kingdom are to have the ultimate priority in our lives.

It is also significant that Jesus tells his disciples that they are to pray for their bread *day by day*. It is as though Jesus is saying that we are not to concern ourselves unduly about security for the distant future, but only the needs we have each day. Common sense and Scripture alike dictate that there be some planning and saving (see 2 Cor. 12:14). But God wants his children to be able to suspend their expectations for future needs on his good providence: 'Therefore do not worry about tomorrow, for tomorrow will worry about its own things. Sufficient for the day is its own trouble' (Matt. 6:34). In this admonition Jesus counsels the 'Live one day at a time' approach. It is sound philosophically and spiritually. God taught the Israelites this principle after their crossing of the Red Sea by supplying *daily* manna. When they tried to hoard it, the manna stank (Exod.16:20).

The longing for security and certainty is one of the most powerful inclinations of human nature. Fundamentally there is nothing wrong with this. Salvation itself is a form of security, security for our ultimate destiny, eternity. But in the end there is only one real security, the promises of God. Nothing in this life is absolutely certain. Health fails, businesses and banks fail and government-sponsored welfare systems fail. But God never fails. His children need constantly, daily, to depend upon him to supply their needs. Every day they should ask him, if not in the exact words of the model prayer, at least in some form or other, to give them what they need.

The Lord's admonitions on the matter of trusting God for material blessings are crystal clear. His disciples are not to worry but to trust God and pray. They are to make heaven, not earth, their goal. They are to strive primarily for a knowledge of God and growth in spiritual maturity, not wealth, power, or fame.

The all-important question is, how do we measure up to this ideal given by the Saviour? I am sure we would all have to agree that God's children, as a rule, are too much perplexed and distracted over the carnal and perishing comforts of this world. Too many of the health problems, too many of the family disputes, even too many of the compromises and divisions in the church have their root in money problems. Let us all pray that the Lord will enable us to put material things in a proper perspective. God's people need to repent of their praying for fine cars, expensive homes and worldly glory, instead of simply praying for their daily bread.

7.
Purity: forgiving and being forgiven

'And forgive us our sins, for we also forgive everyone who is indebted to us' (Luke 11:4).

The final section of the model prayer as given by Luke ends with a strong emphasis on moral concerns. The first part, now under consideration, relates to the matter of restored relationships with God and our fellow man, which involves *forgiveness.* The second section, to be considered in the next chapter, deals with preservation from temptation and evil. In the version of the model prayer which I use there are fifty-nine words altogether. Of these twenty-nine, or about half, deal with the issue of sin in the life of the believer. God puts a high estimate on holiness of life.

The words 'forgive us our sins' show that believers are a confessing and repenting people. Confession of sin is one of the basic elements of true prayer. In all ages God's servants have poured out their souls to God in heartfelt confession and repentance, often with weeping and bitterness of spirit (see Ps. 51; Dan. 9:3-19).

The believer's ongoing struggle with sin

If the Lord had anticipated that his disciples would be free from the problem of sin he certainly would not have incorporated the pro-vision of confession in the model prayer. The faithful record of the conduct of the disciples during our Lord's earthly ministry shows clearly that they were anything but perfect. He was continually admonishing, sometimes even rebuking them, for their shortcom-ings. How candidly the Scriptures record the sins of the apostles of Christ! Peter was very presumptuous and unaware of his own limitations, vehemently denying that he would ever be unfaithful to Christ (Mark 14:31). Eventually he succumbed to a craven fear, even to the point of denying the Lord (Mark 14:68). James and John were intolerant of others and were ready to invoke fiery judgement from heaven on the Samaritans (Luke 9:54). They were also guilty of carnal ambition, as seen by their arguing among themselves as to who would have the pre-eminent position in Christ's kingdom (Mark 10:35-45). Philip demonstrated amazing spiritual blindness and ignorance (John 14:8-9). Thomas was possessed of a foolish unbelief that had to be relieved by a physical demonstration (John 20:24-29). All of the disciples at times were untrusting and fearful.

True believers today are often guilty of the same, or even worse, moral lapses. It is true that the disciples who were under the instruction and discipline of Christ on earth were at this point in an immature condition. Some might conceivably argue that the coming of the Holy Spirit on the church after Christ's ascension leaves no room for sinful conduct. Yet all the writings of the New Testament reveal the plain fact that the saints of God are, as long as they are in the world, still in a struggle with the sins of the flesh. John states bluntly, 'If we say that we have no sin, we deceive ourselves, and the truth is not in us' (1 John 1:8).

The level of real holiness to which a Christian can attain in this world is a matter upon which there have been fierce debates. Some teach that sinless perfection is possible. Others virtually deny progressive sanctification altogether. The truth is no doubt between the two extremes. Jesus Christ held a high standard of discipleship and even admonished his followers to be 'perfect, just as your Father in heaven is perfect' (Matt. 5:48). He characterized his disciples (all of them, not just a few) as those who 'abide in [his] word' and 'follow [him]' (John 8:31; 10:27). Without a doubt such teachings of Jesus are a rebuke to those who make conversion to Christ an insignificant experience, which leaves people still bound by the chains of sin.

On the other hand, the Gospels affirm just as clearly that the followers of Christ still have a nature in which resides the effects of Adam's fall. In a moment of weakness they can become guilty of the same transgressions which dominate the people of the world. They can stray at times from the fold of the Shepherd and become the prey of Satan. The model prayer alone is proof that Jesus knew that his disciples would often need to confess their sins.

It is important to note that the model prayer gives a perfect balance on the difficult issue of sin in the life of the believer. On the one hand, Jesus recognizes the problem and leaves room for confession and forgiveness. Yet God's ideal of holiness is not compromised, for Jesus includes the petition for deliverance from sin. The last petition of the model prayer is: 'Do not lead us into temptation, but deliver us from the evil one.'

The nature of God's forgiveness

There are many loads that God's people are called upon to carry in this life. There is the load of labour and toil, with all its attendant pressures and stress. There is the load of affliction, such as sickness, poverty and bereavement. There is, however, no burden heavier than the burden of sin. The feeling of guilt, caused by the accusing finger of conscience, drives its piercing knife into the human spirit. Even those who have never received Christ as Saviour and Lord do not escape the torment of a guilty conscience. The untold mental and emotional misery that has come by unresolved sin will only be revealed by eternity itself.

False religion capitalizes on the human need for forgiveness by offering this or that remedy. Some groups intentionally hold people in suspense by keeping them dependent on rituals or the ordained clergy for relief for their tormented consciences. Exploitation of guilt can even lead to the making merchandise of the souls of men. We all know about the infamous indulgences sold by Tetzel. Tear-jerking appeals for donations by some American television preachers are sometimes nothing but guilt exploitation. There is no doubt about it, feelings of guilt are real, as can be seen by what some are willing to pay to be rid of it. But guilt needs a true remedy, not an artificial one.

True deliverance from sin comes from God, and it is offered freely without money and without price. God, as we see clearly revealed in Scripture, is a forgiving God. He is willing and able to take away the nagging, knawing torment of guilt, along with all the fears that go with it. 'There is forgiveness with you,' said the psalmist (Ps. 130:4). How we should praise and thank God that it is so!

Forgiveness in Scripture means the restoration of a relationship (usually between two people) based on a removal of the effects of sin. When forgiveness occurs the offended person is no longer resentful and does not consider the offender to be subject to punishment for wrongdoing. Forgiveness certainly involves pardon, but it is more than pardon. When a criminal is pardoned he is delivered from the danger of punishment, but he is still considered a sinner. When God forgives a sinner he not only pardons but legally removes the sin itself. That is the amazing thing about the gospel.

It helps us to understand the meaning of forgiveness when we consider sin as a debt. Both versions of the model prayer represent sin as debt. In fact, in Matthew's version the prayer for forgiveness is 'Forgive us our debts, as we forgive our debtors' (6:12). Luke's version says, 'Forgive us our sins,' but then adds, 'for we also forgive everyone who is indebted to us'. Our sins have made us debtors to God. Forgiveness means that the debt is cancelled or removed. A forgiven person enjoys God's favour and is no longer obligated to pay for sin.

The basis of forgiveness

In human transactions, such as in creditor-debtor relationships, a debt can be removed simply through generosity. In some cases a business simply overlooks or 'forgives' the debt. Since this often happens in human affairs some assume that God forgives in the same way. They believe that God, being a very compassionate and benevolent being, simply overlooks human sin. A blasphemous writer once said, even while denouncing religion, 'God will forgive me . . . it is his business!' The thought seemed to be that God is obligated to forgive; it would be ungodlike for him to do otherwise. Others appear to think that God takes a kind of nonchalant attitude towards human rebellion, much like that of an indulgent parent who when told that his sons were caught stealing says, 'Oh, well, boys will be boys!'

But God does not forgive because he is tolerant or indulgent. The fact is that God cannot and will not forgive without some reparation to the claims of his law. The law of God demands eternal death as the only adequate satisfaction for those who break it (Ezek. 18:4; Rom. 6:23). But God in infinite mercy (not indulgence or tolerance) has provided a way for sinners to be forgiven without the demands of the law being set aside. He sent his Son to die on the cross and pay the full price of sin in a substitutionary way. Because Jesus was God he was able to perform in a few hours on the cross what would be required of sinners in eternal separation from God. Since Jesus satisfied the demands of the law, God is now able to offer forgiveness to all who receive him.

The Scriptures describe the work of Jesus Christ in dying for sin as redemption, which means buying back by paying a price. The One to whom the price was paid was God, since it was his law that was broken. The price itself was Christ's life, as symbolized by his shed blood. Thus we believe in *blood redemption*. It is on the basis of Jesus' death for sinners that God can now offer forgiveness to lost sinners. As Ephesians 1:7 says, 'In him we have redemption through his blood, the forgiveness of sins, according to the riches of his grace.' We receive the benefits of Christ's redemptive work by faith. When a sinner believes what the Bible says concerning Christ and trusts in him fully for salvation, all his sins are forgiven. In this way God forgives in a way consistent with his holiness.

The word for forgiveness in Luke 11:4 *(aphiemi)* comes from two roots meaning 'to send away'. The sins of a believer are 'sent away', or in the words of the prophet, they are cast 'into the depths of the sea' (Micah 7:19). There is a beautiful picture of this in the Old Testament. On the great Day of Atonement the high priest of Israel presented two goats before the Lord at the door of the tabernacle. One of the goats was to be used as an offering for sin. It was killed by the priest and its blood was sprinkled on the mercy seat within the inner sanctuary of the tabernacle. The killing of this goat for a sin offering pictures Jesus Christ as a propitiation for the sins of his people. (Propitiation means that which turns away wrath, 1 John 2:2.)

The other goat, known as a scapegoat, was not killed immediately but was sent away into the wilderness alive. Before it was led into the desert, the priest laid his hands on it, confessing the iniquities of the children of Israel. Following this the goat was led outside the environs of Israel to perish. This animal was 'sent away' into the wilderness (Lev. 16:21). Although we cannot say for sure which wilderness is meant, we do know that to the south of Jerusalem was a mountainous district which was very barren and desolate. There the scapegoat, cut off from water, food and shelter, perished under the blazing oriental sun. What a powerful picture this is of Christ's suffering! Jesus was 'sent away', as it were, into the regions of spiritual death on behalf of sinners. Because he bore the awful load of sin he came under the judicial displeasure of God. Since he was willing to be the scapegoat, all who receive Christ as Saviour and Lord are now released from the burden of sin. Just as symbolically the goat of the atonement day took for ever the sins of Israel into the wilderness, so Jesus took our sins away for ever by paying the debt on Calvary. In Christ our sins have been 'sent away' or forgiven.

When the believer sins he needs only to come to God through Christ, humbly confess his sins and receive God's gracious cleansing. Having asked God to forgive his sins on the basis of Christ's redeeming work, he can now accept by faith that free pardon. He does not need to wonder if really and truly his sins are forgiven. The Scriptures assure us that the heavenly Father is ready and willing to forgive if we only come with sincere confession and repentance. As 1 John 1:9 says, 'If we confess our sins, he is faithful and just to forgive us our sins and to cleanse us from all unrighteousness.'

Practising forgiveness

There is both an active and a passive side to forgiveness in the life of the believer. In the model prayer Jesus makes it clear that an experience of forgiveness through the free grace of God should generate a corresponding attitude of forgiveness towards others. Reconciliation must be two-dimensional: Godward and manward. When God forgives the Christian of his many sins through the redemption of Christ, a proper relationship with God is established. When a Christian, with the gracious example of God always in view, is able to forgive others, a proper relationship with others is established: 'And forgive us our sins, for we also forgive everyone who is indebted to us.'

Jesus Christ often admonished his disciples to forgive one another. On one occasion Peter asked him how often he was obliged to forgive his brother who had sinned against him. Thinking, no doubt, that he was being very generous, he wondered if he should even forgive 'up to seven times' (Matt. 18:21). Jesus answered, 'I do not say to you, up to seven times, but up to seventy times seven' (v. 22). Obviously Jesus is teaching that there is really no limit to the number of times a disciple should be willing to forgive an offending brother.

Following this admonition Jesus gave a parable which was designed to illustrate how the disciples were to reflect and demonstrate God's willingness to forgive. He spoke of a servant who owed a large amount of money to his master and was in danger of being sold into slavery in order to pay. But the master, 'moved with compassion', forgave him the debt (Matt. 18:27). Soon the servant found himself in a somewhat similar situation. A fellow servant owed him a much smaller amount than he had originally owed to his master. The fellow servant fell at his feet and begged for patience in resolving the debt. But his pathetic plea was not heard. The debtor was afforded no mercy and was thrown into prison. Other servants then reported this severity to the master who had originally been owed money. Outraged at this injustice and inconsistency, the master reinstated the servant's debt and 'delivered him to the torturers until he should pay all that was due to him' (v. 34). Jesus drives home the obvious point: it is a travesty when one who expects to be forgiven by God does not show mercy towards his brothers: 'So my heavenly Father also will do to you if each of you, from his heart, does not forgive his brother his trespasses' (v. 35).

The importance of forgiving others is emphasized immediately following the model prayer, as given in the Sermon on the Mount: 'For if you forgive men their trespasses, your heavenly Father will also forgive you. But if you do not forgive men their trespasses, neither will your Father forgive your trespasses' (Matt. 6:14-15). This is strong language. All of us who profess to be disciples of Jesus Christ need to pay careful attention to it.

It is very important to note that Jesus makes God's own faithfulness and goodness in forgiving us the standard of our forgiving others. Those who have received a free and full pardon for their sins from God Almighty should certainly be willing to forgive erring brothers. God, whose holiness has been offended and whose law has been broken, is willing to forgive freely and fully guilty sinners, even the vilest, if they will come to him through the blood of his Son. He, who has every right to dispatch anyone and everyone to the flames of eternal hell, is willing to wipe the slate clean. What an inconsistency it is when someone who claims to have benefited from God's goodness demonstrates a harsh and intolerant attitude towards others.

The language in which Jesus demands a forgiving spirit is solemn and searching. He says that anyone who does not forgive cannot himself be forgiven. This does not mean that our forgiveness of others is the *ground* of our being forgiven, for, as we have seen, this can only come about by faith in Christ's atonement. Neither does this mean that our forgiveness is the *measure* of God's forgiveness of us. He forgives perfectly, while everything in us is imperfect. What it does mean is that it is utterly hypocritical for anyone to ask God for forgiveness while at the same time he is harbouring an unforgiving spirit himself. The person whose spirit is so narrow and resentful that he cannot release his brother from a moral debt cannot expect God to forgive him. That, very simply, is the lesson given here.

The question may be asked, 'Should we forgive those who have not acknowledged their sins and expressed regret for them?' There seems to be a difference between flagrant, obvious violations of God's law and offences which are based more or less on human weaknesses. As to the former we cannot, as agents of the gospel, be indifferent to open rebellion against God. Forgiveness in such cases clearly requires repentance. But many of the causes of offence in human relationships relate to slights and inconveniences which should simply be overlooked. That is no doubt what Jesus had in mind when he admonished the disciples to 'turn the other cheek' (Matt. 5:39).

Jesus is teaching that, in its extreme form, an unforgiving spirit is inconsistent with a genuine experience of conversion. He is warning that someone who cannot forgive his brother has a spirit that is totally foreign to the very spirit of the gospel. Although any of God's children can, at times, be guilty of harbouring resentment and ill-will, Jesus is clearly showing the dangerous consequences of such a spirit. Persistent, inveterate, unbending, callous ill-will towards others cannot reside for ever in the bosom of one of God's children. As C. H. Spurgeon put it (in a message on Ephesians 4:32), 'You must forgive or you cannot be saved.'

The teachings of Christ on repentance, confession and forgiveness are a sound basis for reconciliation and harmony in all levels of human society. When the followers of Christ are able, even in a small measure, to partake of the generous forgiving spirit of their Lord, what a difference it makes! Old wounds in family relationships are healed. Painful ruptures in the church are repaired, or even prevented. It is because the teachings of Christ on forgiveness are so little practised that the world in which we live is a scene of incessant strife and alienation.

Let those of us who profess to follow Jesus Christ do what we can to promote peace among our fellow men by practising the teachings of our Saviour on forgiving others. Let us seek, whenever we are harmed and offended by others, ever to look at Calvary's cross, where God demonstrated his marvellous forgiving mercy towards us. On the basis of that example, let us be ready to forgive our erring neighbours and brothers, even to seventy times seven.

8.
Preservation: deliverance from sin

'And do not lead us into temptation, but deliver us from the evil one'
(Luke 11:4).

When believers pray for forgiveness they are praying for the removal of the problems in relationships that sin causes. A forgiven person is one who is restored to fellowship with God. But this is not the only concern of God's children. They not only wish to have past sins washed away through the blood of Christ; they also wish to be preserved from future sins. The gospel provides for deliverance not only from the *penalty* of sin, but from the *power* of sin as well.

God's people are to be a holy people

The word for temptation in our text has two meanings. Sometimes it has reference to a trial or affliction. So it is used in 1 Peter 4:12, where it is translated 'fiery trial'. A trial is anything that puts us to the test. The difficulties of life, such as sickness, poverty and bereavement, certainly put the believer to a test. Our faith and submission to God are tried when such things happen. Is Jesus saying that we should ask God that we should not be subjected to the innumerable afflictions which come upon people in this world? It is certainly not wrong that we pray that we may be saved from the sufferings of this life, if it is God's will. That does not seem to be the meaning here, however.

Temptation also means in Scripture inducement or enticement to evil. A temptation in that sense is an occasion for sin — a moral test. So it means in Luke 4:2, where we read that Jesus was 'tempted' for forty days by the devil. By including the prayer, 'Lead us not into temptation,' Jesus is obviously teaching the disciples that they are to seek God's help in avoiding inducements to sin, and above all sin itself. They are, in other words, to pray for holiness.

A substantial part of Jesus' instructions to the disciples deals specifically with their walk of obedience. The experience of salvation which Christ's gospel brings is a scheme of salvation by divine mercy and grace. There is nothing that men can do to merit salvation or secure it by their own efforts. But how is God's saving grace displayed in this world? The answer is obvious. God's power and grace are demonstrated by their operation in the lives of those who have been saved. Jesus taught his disciples that their changed lives, more than anything else, vindicated the claims of the gospel.

It would be an interesting study to examine the recorded messages of Jesus Christ to his disciples and see how much emphasis he put upon their obedience. The Sermon on the Mount, probably the most well-known and thoroughly studied of all Jesus' messages, deals almost exclusively with the attitudes and conduct which should characterize those who follow him. This sermon is about purity of heart (Matt. 5:8), 'good works' (v. 16), 'righteousness' (v. 20) and the avoidance of anger (v. 22), lust (v. 28) and selfishness (vv. 41, 42). Above all this sermon teaches that the followers of Christ are to be a loving people. They are even to love their enemies and pray for those who persecute them (v.44).

In demanding of his disciples a life of faithfulness, service and love, Jesus is only echoing a theme which runs throughout the Scriptures: God's demand that his people be a holy people. God gave his law to Israel through Moses. To Moses God said, 'Speak to all the congregation of the children of Israel, and say to them: "You shall be holy, for I the Lord your God am holy"' (Lev. 19:2). The holiness God demanded of Israel was not just a sterile outward separation from certain external vices (though it included that), but a true loyalty and devotion to the God who had chosen them as a nation and called them to be a special people unto him. Above all it meant avoiding idolatry, the ever present problem for a people surrounded by nations that knew not their God.

When the redeemed people of God walk in obedience and avoid the temptations of a perishing world, God is glorified. So Jesus taught his disciples in these words: 'Let your light so shine before men, that they may see your good works and glorify your Father in heaven' (Matt. 5:16). The people of the world judge the power of a religion by the conduct of its adherents. It brings shame to the cause of truth when the professed followers of Jesus are selfish, arrogant, lustful and covetous. But when faith in God produces the opposite character traits of love, humility, chastity and generosity, it recommends the gospel to those who have not received it. Obedient Christians glorify the power of God, because they show that grace can conquer man's natural rebellious heart. Obedient Christians glorify the wisdom of God, because by their faithfulness they contribute to a happier and more stable world. Obedient Christians glorify the love of God, for by demonstrating kindness and mercy towards their fellow men they reflect the mercy that ultimately comes from God.

The power of temptation and the weakness of the flesh

A lot is at stake as believers weigh issues of right and wrong and pray for deliverance from temptation. Their conduct reflects on the character of God. The integrity of their profession depends on obedience. Yet the solemn fact is that the road to godly living is a difficult one. In fact it would be better to say that this road is, from the standpoint of human abilities, an impossible one. It is only by the grace of God that even the true followers of Christ are able to avoid falling into the snare of temptation. Just as the natural man cannot come to Christ without the gracious drawing of the Father (John 6:44), so it is impossible for the Christian to live a life of consecration without the continued assistance of his heavenly Father. If obedience came easily, if holiness were a simple and natural thing, then Jesus would not insist that his disciples plead with the Father that they should not be led into temptation.

In the previous chapter we noted that the disciples who were the first followers of Christ demonstrated only too graphically how imperfect they were. They were prone to fearfulness, pride, intolerance, ignorance and unbelief. Even under the watchful eye and in the sovereign presence of Jesus Christ himself, they still constantly had to be helped and encouraged to press on in their faithfulness. The reason temptation is so real and and the difficulty of holiness so great is the power of a residual sinful nature in the believer.

On one occasion Jesus said to his disciples, 'Watch and pray, lest you enter into temptation. The spirit indeed is willing, but the flesh is weak' (Matt. 26:41). The particular temptation or test before the disciples at this time was the greatest one of all. Jesus was about to be betrayed and turned over to his enemies. His arrest, trial and crucifixion were at hand. It was a dark and dismal hour. The storm that had been gathering against Jesus was finally about to break in its fury. Although the disciples were not totally aware of all that was about to occur, they knew from Jesus' warnings that a terrible trial was upon them. They must have watched with great consternation the deep distress which came upon their Master. Although they did not know it at the time, they were in imminent danger of deserting their Lord in order to escape personal injury. They were soon to be tempted to abandon their profession.

The situation the disciples faced as Jesus stood on the brink of his death illustrates why temptation is so fierce. It is because of the weakness of the flesh. Jesus knew that they really loved him and in their hearts did not wish to be fickle followers. 'The spirit is willing,' he acknowledged. The new nature of the believer, the higher self which is subject to the will of God, is 'willing' to do right, even to the point of sacrificing personal interests for the Saviour. But, alas, every child of God also contends with another element in his personality known as 'the flesh'. The flesh is the sinful tendency of human nature which is inherited by birth. It refers to the old desires and ambitions which yearn for selfish pleasure, power and safety. That part of the believer's constitution is notoriously 'weak'. When the disciples yield to the dictates of the flesh they always fall. Jesus knew that if the flesh prevailed in the present situation they would skulk away into the shadows when faced with the call for loyalty in a time of danger. That is exactly what happened.

There is within the child of God a never-ending struggle between these two principles mentioned by Jesus Christ: the spirit and the flesh. In a time of temptation, when there is strong inducement or enticement towards evil, both principles come into operation automatically. The spirit counsels resistance to temptations, but the flesh counsels compliance. The spirit inclines the believer to place the honour of the Lord and a clear conscience above all. The flesh constrains the believer to cast conscience and principle aside and do what is gratifying for the moment. The tension between the spirit and the flesh is fierce and painful, the more so if the temptation involves a blatant, overt act of infidelity to the commandments of Christ.[1]

If we take into consideration how important it is that believers glorify and honour their Lord by standing against the sinful motions of the mind and flesh, we can understand how essential it is that they pray continually, 'Lead us not into temptation.' The use of this prayer is an acknowledgement of the need for personal holiness and also it is a frank recognition of the weakness of the flesh. The fiercer the temptation and the greater the consciousness of personal weakness, the more urgent the need for the prayer. Since there is within the heart of every true follower of Jesus a desire to honour and please him, all of them are deeply interested in the resources for victory over the flesh. In the battle against sin and the pursuit of holiness, prayer is the greatest resource.

How does God 'lead' people into temptation?

If it is a part of the believer's duty to pray that God will deliver him from temptation, then the implication is that God does have some control over circumstances surrounding temptation. If we are to request that God does not lead us into temptation, does this mean that the possibility exists that he can and will at times do just that? We know that as a perfectly holy being God hates sin in all forms. We also know that he cannot be tempted nor does he tempt anyone (James 1:13). But if God does not tempt why should we pray that he should not 'lead' us into temptation?

This question relates to the subject of God's sovereignty and the origin of evil. Can God prevent sin in the lives of free agents? Could he have prevented Adam's sin which brought ruin and condemnation upon the human race? This is a favourite subject with systematic theologians and frankly the whole theme has been the occasion of much speculation and frequently some unprofitable discussion. David resolved,

> 'Lord, my heart is not haughty,
> Nor my eyes lofty,
> Neither do I concern myself with great matters,
> Nor with things too profound for me'
>
> (Ps. 131:1).

The relation of God's sovereignty and power to human evil is, like the truth of the Trinity, one of the deep mysteries which defy human explanation. There are definite limits to how far human speculation can go in this area.

The Bible does not seek to answer directly many of the questions that relate to God's power and the existence of evil. We do find revealed in Scripture, however, that God is able so to manage the universe that sin is overruled for his own glory and honour. It would be foolhardy, indeed even blasphemous, to deny that God can prevent sin. In fact there are instances in Scripture where God is specifically said to have kept people from sinning. God said to Abimelech after he nearly defiled Sarah, 'I also withheld you from sinning against me' (Gen. 20:6). If God prevented sin in this instance, he could certainly prevent it in any instance. Such verses surely show us that God sometimes prevents, and at other times permits, evil.

The Scriptures teach that God's sovereign control extends even to the realms of Satan's activity and human rebellion. It was by God's permission that Satan's fury was unleashed against Job (Job 2:6). All events of time and history, including even the devil's activities, are subject to God's providential direction. This being the case, we can lay it down as a fundamental principle that all circumstances, including temptations to evil, are within the scope of God's permissive purpose. There is, therefore, no great difficulty in interpreting the prayer, 'Do not lead us into temptation.' This is simply a prayer that God, in his infinite and undeserved goodness, should not allow us to be subjected to situations which tempt us beyond our endurance. As John A. Broadus says in his *Commentary on Matthew*, 'The thought here is of God's so ordering things in his providence as to bring us into trying circumstances, which would put our principles and characters to the test. This providential action does not compel us to do wrong, for such conditions become to us the occasion of sin only when our own evil desires are the impelling cause.' Even if God should see fit to permit us to be tried or tempted by inducements to evil, he cannot be charged with sin, for that comes from the deliberate choice of free agents.

Prayer for deliverance from evil

Deliverance from temptation is the first line of defence against sin. After all, prevention is better than cure. But the model prayer also provides for dealing with sin after it happens. First there must be forgiveness through God's mercy in Christ. Then there should be a striving for victory over the power of sin. The words, 'but deliver us from the evil one,' show that not just pardon but victory should be the goal of the believer. Although these words are not included in some translations of Luke's version of the model prayer they are unquestionably in Matthew and will be considered in this study.[2]

The older versions say, 'Deliver us from evil,' whereas some newer ones translate this prayer: 'Deliver us from the evil one.' Either translation is possible. If the former is true the prayer is for salvation from sin as moral defilement. If the latter is correct the prayer is for deliverance from Satan, who is the evil one. Since throughout Luke the Greek word here is used for evil, not Satan, I prefer the former interpretation.

What is it to be delivered from sin? What can God's children reasonably expect in the way of salvation from evil in this world? Such questions must be asked if we are to learn exactly what our Lord had in mind in this prayer.

Salvation or deliverance from sin (they mean the same thing in Scripture) is threefold. First, the believer has been delivered from the *penalty* of sin through the merits of Jesus Christ. The claims of God's law have already been satisfied in the person of Jesus Christ, so that all who are in him are no longer exposed to its judgements. Jesus referred to this aspect of salvation in John 5:24: 'Most assuredly, I say to you, he who hears my word and believes in him who sent me has everlasting life, and shall not come into judgement, but has passed from death into life.' A sinner who has believed in Jesus Christ is no longer under the sentence of condemnation because Christ's righteousness is imputed to him and his death has released him from sin's wages. This aspect of salvation is known as *justification*. This is a once for all event which takes place at conversion. It admits of no degrees and is final. The believer is as justified at the time he accepts the gospel as he will be in heaven.

Jesus is clearly not speaking of justification when he provides that believers pray, 'Deliver us from evil.' That is already a settled fact, a blessing which happened immediately at conversion. Justification simply needs to be claimed by faith.

This prayer refers to the second aspect of salvation which is deliverance from the *power* of sin, which is known as *sanctification*. Sanctification, unlike justification, admits of degrees. It is not final and complete at conversion but is progressive and conditional. To be sanctified means to be 'set apart' unto God. As the believer's love grows (2 Thess. 1:3), and faith grows (1 Thess. 3:10), and hope grows (Rom. 15:13), he becomes more and more set apart unto God.

Most of the terms used to describe the Christian life suggest progress. This is true of running the race (Heb. 12:1), adding to our faith (2 Peter 1:5) and growing in grace and in the knowledge of our Lord and Saviour (2 Peter 3:18). Jesus compared the experience of the believer to a seed which is planted in the ground. There is the sprouting, the growing and finally the yielding of the crop, which itself is progressive — the blade, the head and then the full grain (Mark 4:27-28).

It is fairly easy to see how the positive side of sanctification (growth in faith, love and hope) is progressive, but it is not so easy to see how the negative side, deliverance from sin, is progressive. The Christian often seems, in his own eyes, to be getting worse, not better. Yet a growing consciousness and sensitivity to sin is itself an evidence of progress and maturity. The closer we get to the light, the more we see the dirt on us. So the closer we get to Christ, the more we lament our sin.

The *Westminster Confession of Faith* teaches that by virtue of Christ's death and resurrection and through the indwelling of the Holy Spirit the power of sin can be 'weakened and mortified' (ch. 13, section 1). This document is not teaching the eradication of the old nature or even that there is any essential change in the principle of indwelling sin. It simply recognizes the marvellous provision God has made for us in the Holy Spirit's sanctifying work. When a Christian's heart and life are controlled by the Holy Spirit, he or she will not 'fulfil the lust of the flesh' (Gal. 5:16). To deny that believers can overcome sin as a prevailing influence is to minimize the greatness of God's power working in them.

The final aspect of salvation is deliverance from the *presence* of sin. At the resurrection the Christian will receive a new body and a soul purged from all taint of sin. Then will be fulfilled in a perfect and final way the prayer, 'Deliver us from evil.' Although this is, I believe, not the primary intent in this prayer, it may well be included.

I am afraid that the part of the model prayer which deals with holiness is too often passed over by professing Christians today. Most of them seem to be more occupied with their own happiness and safety than with personal godliness. It is certain that if more people were praying that they should not be led into temptation there would be less moral compromise in the church. Who can doubt that if the church would pray more for deliverance from sin God would hear them?

1. Paul describes this struggle theoretically in Galatians 5:16-26 and personally in Romans 7:13-25.

2. Most of the oldest manuscripts do not contain these words in Luke's version.

9.
Persistence: praying without giving up

'And he said to them, "Which of you shall have a friend, and go to him at midnight and say to him, 'Friend, lend me three loaves; for a friend of mine has come to me on his journey, and I have nothing to set before him'; and he will answer from within and say, 'Do not trouble me; the door is now shut, and my children are with me in bed; I cannot rise and give to you'? I say to you, though he will not rise and give to him because he is his friend, yet because of his persistence he will rise and give him as many as he needs"' (Luke 11:5-8).

We leave now the *model* which Jesus gives in order to teach the disciples how to pray, and proceed to look at the picture or *illustration* of prayer. It comes in the form of the parable quoted above.

A parable has been defined as 'a story in which things in the spiritual realm are compared with events that could happen in the temporal realm; or, an earthly story with a heavenly meaning'.[1] Usually a parable would be an imaginary story, although one in which some of the details actually did take place. The parables of Jesus were taken from customs and circumstances with which his hearers were familiar. Everyone in Jesus' day knew about such practices as sowing and reaping, caring for sheep and attending weddings, which Jesus used to illustrate truth in parabolic form. The purpose of parables was to make very clear the ideas Jesus was putting forth. Usually the parables of Jesus were given to clarify or illustrate *one* main lesson.

It is important, in interpreting parables, that we distinguish between the central part of the parable and incidental details. Parts of the parables serve only for the 'ornamentation' of the parable, and do not relate to the substance. For example, in the parable we are now considering, obviously Jesus is teaching the disciples that they should persist in asking God for blessings even though the answer might not come at once. That is the substance of the parable. The fact that the man asked for 'three' loaves is incidental to the spiritual point. We should not try to find some hidden meaning in this, such as that there are 'three' great spiritual qualities the Christian should seek: faith, hope and love.

It is interesting that of the fifty parables which Jesus gave, two deal specifically with prayer. And there is one great truth that Jesus emphasizes in both of these two parables: the fact that the person who prays should not become discouraged and give up but should continue to ask God for blessings. Jesus taught that we are to persist, not desist. This is the element in prayer which Jesus highlights in the parable of the importunate widow in Luke 18:1-8. Luke introduces this parable by the statement: 'Then he spoke a parable to them, that men always ought to pray and not lose heart.' In the parable a woman succeeds in obtaining a legal settlement from an 'unjust judge' by doggedly persisting in coming to him with her need. The judge ignored her at first but finally, worn out as it were with her pestering, he gave her what she wanted. The lesson of the parable was that if an unjust judge would give a poor widow what she wanted simply to get rid of her, surely our loving heavenly Father will grant his children their requests if they continue to plead with him.

Let us look now at the parable of the importunate friend. Jesus tells of a man who is called upon to entertain a friend, probably a close acquaintance, who is visiting him. Since there was no public accommodation, such as the hotels we have in our modern world, it was expected that a person would find lodging in someone's private home, preferably that of a friend. In the Orient, hospitality was considered a cardinal virtue and great pains were taken to entertain guests with kindness and courtesy. An Oriental proverb says, 'Every stranger is an invited guest.' It was the custom when guests came for the host or hostess to bow, greet them with a salutation, such as 'Peace be on you', kiss them and even wash their feet. Honourable people took great pride in their hospitality.

The visitor Jesus speaks of in the parable evidently had dropped in unexpectedly. There was nothing really unusual about this. He was a 'friend' and had no doubt expected that the usual courtesies would be extended to him. The host, however, faced an embarrassing situation. His cupboards were bare and there was nothing to serve. His honour was at stake. He needed to find a way to show hospitality to his friend. Since it was late in the evening, no market was open to relieve his need. He then did the only thing he could: he went to his neighbour and asked for a loan of three loaves. The neighbour was obviously annoyed by this intrusion into his home at such an hour. 'Do not trouble me; the door is now shut, and my children are with me in bed,' he protested. 'I cannot rise and give to you.'

The host, however, was undaunted. He kept on rapping at the door, begging for help. At last he was successful. 'I say to you,' Jesus concludes, 'though he will not rise and give to him because he is his friend, yet because of his persistence he will rise and give him as many as he needs' (Luke 11:8). Obviously the man in bed concluded that it would be easier and simpler to respond and give the bread than be worried by the incessant pleas outside.

The lesson is obvious. In the simple framework of the parable the sleeping neighbour represents God. The host who pleads at his door represents the believer. The guest and the host's empty pantry represent any real need which a believer may have. In other words, when the child of God pleads for blessings from his heavenly Father he is like a man seeking assistance from a neighbour.

The need

The beautiful thing about this parable is the fact that it is broad and general enough to cover any situation. The host needed bread to feed his guest. He was 'up against it', so to speak. The embarrassingly empty cupboard forced him to seek help from someone else. It must have been hard for him to trudge through the darkness of night and disturb a neighbour. But he had no choice. He was helpless.

We as Christians can put ourselves into the situation of the destitute host. Often when a need arises in our lives we can find some way, through our own resources or ingenuity, to meet the need. But occasionally we look into our cupboard, so to speak, to find the solution to a problem and find it as barren as can be. There is simply nothing we can humanly do to deal with the difficulty. We look to the right and to the left for help, and there is none. No human hand can do anything for us. It is in such situations that we go to our heavenly Father and pound at the door of heaven.

About twenty years ago a nurse gave me some marvellous news

in the waiting room of a hospital: I was now the father of a bouncing baby boy. A girl had been born three years earlier, so now I had my 'million dollar family'. I expected that in three or four days I would be able to take my wife and my new baby home. But things did not go well with my wife. She began to lose blood and was becoming increasingly pale. The doctor who delivered my son had left on a trip and the nurses seemed perplexed as to what to do.

Needless to say, I was deeply concerned. I was a young pastor of a growing church and the father of a three-year-old girl. What would I do if Reta did not get better? I remember well falling on my face in prayer on my bedroom floor. In my mind I seemed to be sailing on a ship through a stormy ocean, and the ship was leaking. So much depended on having my wife at my side. What would I do if she died? I applied to the Lord at this most desperate hour. I begged my gracious heavenly Father, who had given me my wife seven years previously (after many years of praying for a godly companion), to spare her life. It was a time of great trauma and urgency for me. In his great mercy God heard my prayer. Another resident doctor was called in and performed surgery. The operation was successful and my wife's life was saved. I had a need and I took that need to the One who could meet it. Whatever our want, we can take it to God in prayer.

The delay

The parable pictures the neighbour as showing an indifference at first to the request of the man outside. 'The door is shut, the children are in bed, I cannot rise,' he shouts. Jesus is certainly not teaching that there is a callous indifference in the heart of our God for his people. The point is that the host did not quickly succeed in his request. The situation was very discouraging. He received a rebuff that was anything but reassuring. It appeared for a while that he would go away without the three loaves and his guest would have to go to bed hungry.

So it is in the prayer struggles of the believer. He has what he believes is an urgent need. He pleads with his heavenly Father to intervene in his situation. He earnestly, fervently, continually comes to him with a prayer for relief. But nothing happens. The pain persists. The broken home does not mend. The hoped for opportunity does not materialize. The painful temptation does not go away. The unconverted person does not change. All of this in spite of deeply sincere prayers, perhaps even mingled with fasting and tears.

Very frequently what appears to be a lack of success in prayer becomes itself an additional problem. At first there is simply frustration. The believer seeks to submit to his heavenly Father's will, and in a measure does so. He reads in the Bible that he must wait on the Lord, and so he waits. But the need just does not go away. Then frustration sets in. He finds himself asking, 'Why?' 'Why will the Lord not hear me?' he asks. 'I have confessed my sins. I have submitted to his will, as best as I can. Yet he knows the desperate need I have. God has the power to change my circumstances. He says he loves me. Then why am I denied an answer?'

Lack of success in prayer is sometimes not only followed by frustration, but even doubt. The suffering Christian, his stock of patience dangerously low, begins to question himself. Am I really a Christian? What terrible sin have I committed that God will not hear me? He may even question the goodness of God or the inspiration of the Scriptures. 'Maybe the promises of the Bible are not true after all,' something whispers in his ear.

It is in just such a situation that the Lord reminds us, by this simple, but powerful parable, that *we should persist in prayer*. The neighbour won his cause by continually coming, just as the widow finally prevailed upon the judge to vindicate her cause (Luke 18:1-8). To the suffering, fainting, discouraged, desperate believer, Jesus Christ has one message: keep on praying.

The success

Although the host was given a stiff rebuff when he first knocked at the neighbour's door, he eventually came away with his bread. He must have felt a real sense of satisfaction as he made his way back to his waiting guest. Now, at last, he would be able to entertain him. He had 'prevailed' upon his neighbour.

What a joyful thing it is when the believer is able to touch the heart of God and prevail with him in prayer! The satisfaction is all the sweeter when it is some great and wonderful blessing for which he has been pleading and the time of travail in prayer has been long.

Both the judge in Luke 18 and the sleeping neighbour in Luke 11 are represented as reluctant to give, simply because of personal indifference. But what a contrast there is between hard-hearted people upon whom we are often dependent and God! Jesus is clearly seeking to *contrast* the unjust judge and our gracious heavenly Father: 'Then the Lord said, "Hear what the unjust judge said. And shall God not avenge his own elect who cry out day and night to him, though he bears long with them?"' (Luke 18:6-7). If we might paraphrase this, Jesus is saying, 'If the unjust judge, who did not fear God nor regard man, was willing to respond to the poor widow, how much more will God hear his chosen people who plead with him!' Similarly, in the parable of the neighbour Jesus is saying, 'If a selfish neighbour is willing finally to rise from his bed and give someone bread simply because of his persistence, how much more will God give a sympathetic ear to his suffering children, who cry out to him in their deep need!'

Why is it that the answers to prayer sometimes delay so long? To put it another way, why does God make us 'wait', as it were, to shower upon us the blessings we wish? He has the power to relieve our wants very quickly. Why does he not do so?

There is no doubt that frequently God suspends blessings for which we have long prayed simply to test our faith and perseverance in prayer. It would be easy to go through the Bible and show that this is true. God promised to Abraham and Sarah that they would have a son, but a period of some twenty-five years elapsed before the blessing actually came. Even after Isaac was born, Abraham's loyalty to God and patience were sorely tested when God commanded him to take his son Isaac and offer him on Mount Moriah for a sacrifice. The long years that intervened must have been sorely trying to the patriarch and his wife. They became so frustrated and impatient that they even took matters into their own hands and arranged that Abraham's slave Hagar bear him a son. This was, of course, a terrible mistake, for which they paid dearly. But in regard to the waiting period and to the command to offer up Isaac, both these ordeals were to demonstrate Abraham's faith and obedience. Genesis 22:1 says, 'Now it came to pass after these things that God tested Abraham.' After his obedience in offering to sacrifice his son, God said to Abraham, 'Now I know that you fear God since you have not withheld your son, your only son, from me' (Gen. 22:12).

It takes faith on the part of the believer to pray, pray, pray for a long period of time and trust God to keep his promises, even when there is no visible evidence of hope. It takes a submissive spirit for a person to lie helpless and empty before the feet of our sovereign God and call upon him continually for relief from some vexing problem, especially when God is not pleased to intervene and change the situation quickly. Yet God is honoured by such persistence. In fact the graces of patience, submission and trust are brought to light by the delay in receiving answers to prayer. Above all, the seriousness of our commitment to obtaining the blessing is tested when we must wait and wait for prayer to be answered.

As a matter of personal testimony, I must say that many of my really significant blessings have come after many years of seeking them from God. I mentioned earlier about how the Lord healed my wife through a physician. This took place in a short period of time. But it has not always happened this way. Events of personal triumph over various difficulties, some involving gospel ministry, have come after long years of praying and waiting. Often I have prayed for help from God in an area of my life and received time and time again the answer, 'No.' Doors simply would not open. Often have I experienced the truth of Proverbs 13:12: 'Hope deferred makes the heart sick.' Yet the verse continues, 'But when the desire comes, it is a tree of life.' Yes, our fervent desires, shared in faith and submission to our God, often seem to be like a dead trunk of a tree, lifeless and barren. But God can revive our spirits by giving life to our hopes and the realized dreams are like a 'tree of life'.

There is no doubt about it, God's children tend to give up too easily in their applications for God's help in the struggles of life. Our Saviour made it clear that God wants us, God expects us, to keep on asking, keep on seeking and keep on knocking. Especially when our prayers relate to the Christian warfare, we need to be persistent. When we are seeking to win souls to salvation, when we are standing against error, when we are seeking to build up the kingdom of God in our communities, we need to press on, not only in preaching and teaching, but also in praying. The Bible is filled with promises that God will reward the patient, praying warrior for him:

'Therefore the Lord will wait,
  that he may be gracious to you.
And therefore he may be exalted,
  that he may have mercy on you.

For the Lord is a God of justice;
Blessed are all those who wait for him'

                                                    (Isa. 30:18).

Intercessory prayer

It may seem at first glance that nothing is said about intercessory prayer in Luke 11. But if we look a little more closely we can see that Jesus does indeed include this element in his teachings. For one thing, in the phrase, 'For we also forgive everyone who is indebted to us,' the need for intercessory praying is implied. It is impossible to pray for someone and hold a grudge at the same time. Forgiveness and intercession go hand in hand. Forgiveness of others and prayers for them should intertwine and support one another. Intercessory prayer cannot be sustained in the stifling air of hatred. Forgiveness will not thrive in the barren soil of prayerlessness.

It is significant, perhaps, though I would not wish to press the point, that in the Luke 11 parable on persistence, it is on behalf of someone else that the host goes to his neighbour for bread. The host is concerned about his travel-weary and hungry guest. He has already enjoyed, in all probability, a meal for himself and his children. It is just that there is not enough now to serve anyone else. Even so the Christian is standing on high ground indeed when his prayers of persistence are sent to God on behalf of other needy people. When we are praying for the lost to be saved, when we are praying for ministers to preach with power, when we pray for the removal of obstacles faced by a missionary, when we pray for healing for some sick sister in Christ, then especially we need to pray perseveringly. We need to stand knocking at God's door till he opens and gives us the bread.

1. *Handy Dictionary of the Bible*

10.
Promises: encouragement to pray in faith

'And I say to you, ask, and it will be given to you; seek, and you will find; knock, and it will be opened to you. For everyone who asks receives, and he who seeks finds, and to him who knocks it will be opened' (Luke 11:9-10).

There are many sources of encouragement in Holy Scripture for believers to pray with confidence and assurance that their prayers will be answered. Three have been particularly important to me. I have always kept these matters before me in my own prayer life.

First, *the gracious character of God* is revealed in the Bible as a comforting basis for confidence in prayer. God is represented in Scripture as able and willing to shower blessings down upon his creatures on earth. As the psalmist puts it so graphically,

'The Lord is gracious and full of compassion,
Slow to anger and great in mercy.
The Lord is good to all,
And his tender mercies are over all his works'

(Ps. 145:8-9).

The expression, 'The Lord is good to all,' is interesting. The largesse of the great Creator extends not only to his redeemed people, but even to those who do not love and serve him. This is amazing when one considers that many of those who benefit from the goodness of God do not return to him the praise that is due to him, or even acknowledge his existence.

Jesus taught that God's amazing benignity and providential kindness even to his enemies is a pattern for the attitude believers are to have towards others. He admonishes them to love their enemies, bless those who curse them, do good to those who hate them and pray for those who persecute them, 'that you may be sons of your Father in heaven; for he makes his sun rise on the evil and on the good, and sends rain on the just and the unjust' (Matt. 5:45). God's sun warms the body even of the atheist. His rain falls on the fields even of those who hate him. If God is so bountiful to all his creation, how much more willing he surely is to bestow blessings on his own children! Truly, 'The eyes of the Lord are on the righteous, and his ears are open to their prayers' (1 Peter 3:12).

The second source of encouragement to pray with confidence is *the many examples of answered prayer in the Bible*. Let anyone read through the Scriptures and take careful note of the instances in which Bible characters made requests from God, and he will see that in most cases God gave them exactly what they asked for. Jacob asked God to deliver him from the cruel revenge of his brother Esau, and he did (Gen. 32). The nation of Israel sought from God a way of escape from Pharaoh's hosts, and he delivered them (Exod. 14). Hannah, broken-hearted because she was childless, earnestly pleaded with God for a son, and soon she received this gift (1 Sam.1). The list could go on and on. In response to prayer David was delivered from his fears (Ps. 34:4), Jabez saw his territory enlarged (1 Chron. 4:10), Jehoshaphat was rescued from a formidable host of pagans (2 Chron. 20), Hezekiah s life was lengthened (2 Kings 20), and Peter was freed from prison (Acts 12).

The promises of Jesus

The life and ministry of Jesus Christ dramatically illustrate the glorious truth that coming to God for help — any kind of help — meets with success. In his travels up and down the land of Palestine, not only in his native Galilee but also in Samaria and Judea, Jesus was constantly beset with requests for help for a multitude of problems. The lame, the deaf, the blind, the paralysed, the leprous and the demon-possessed — along with many more — were healed by him when they came and prayed to him: 'Now Jesus went about all Galilee . . . healing all kinds of sickness and all kinds of disease among the people' (Matt. 4:23). When parents asked for their ailing children to be delivered, he responded with his miraculous healing power (Mark 7:24-30; John 4:46-54); Jesus even raised people from the dead on three occasions (Luke 7:11-17; 8:40-56; John 11:38-44). While recognizing that Jesus Christ is not here on earth now, performing such astounding miracles, we can assume, since he is 'the same yesterday, today, and for ever,' that he looks sympathetically upon his suffering children.

The third source of encouragement in prayer is *the many promises of Scripture which specifically state that God hears and answers prayer.* Such promises are not hard to find in the Scriptures, but are everywhere. Like ripe apples on the low branches in an orchard, they are close at hand, ready to be plucked. Wise is the Christian who not only is constantly looking for such promises, but has the faith to take them.

Our study is primarily about the teachings of Jesus Christ on the subject of prayer. Precious indeed, and numerous, are the places where Jesus promises to reward the praying believer. The promise at the head of this chapter is certainly one of the most encouraging admonitions to pray in all of Holy Scripture: 'Ask, and it will be given to you; seek, and you will find; knock, and it will be opened to you,' said the Saviour. Here is a promise in triplicate, so worded as to provide the maximum incentive to the child of God, even the weakest and most fearful, to pray with confidence.

The three verbs used by Jesus to describe prayer are themselves interesting: 'ask,' 'seek' and 'knock'. These are all action words designed to describe graphically what prayer is. They suggest that the person who is serious about praying should have his whole soul engaged, just as someone who is in pursuit of some material benefit uses every physical and mental faculty. Asking is an action of the lips. Seeking is an action of the eyes. Knocking is an action of the hands. Spiritually speaking, the Christian is to use them all as he applies to his heavenly Father for the blessings he so desperately wants. He is to 'ask' or to 'present his case' to the Lord (Isa. 41:21). He is to 'seek' out the promises of God and use them as arguments in prayer. He is to 'knock' at the door of heaven, confidently expecting that his Father will come and admit him into the house of rich reward.

Jesus, who is God and cannot lie, says that those who ask receive, those who seek find and those who knock will certainly see an opening door. There is a certain, infallible and necessary connection between the human action of asking and the divine response of giving. One is conditional on the other. While God is 'good to all' and reserves the right to bestow his mercies wherever and whenever and on whomever he pleases, it is those who come enquiring from God who can expect to have a cup overflowing with blessings. It is certainly carnal presumption to expect to receive without asking. But also it is criminal unbelief to ask without expecting to receive.

The 'ask, seek, knock' passage (which appears in almost identical form in Matthew 7:7-8) is only one of the many powerful promises Jesus gives to encourage his disciples to be mighty in prayer. In Mark 11:22-24 Jesus affirms that spiritual mountains can be moved by believing prayer: 'So Jesus answered and said to them, "Have faith in God. For assuredly, I say to you, whoever says to this mountain, 'Be removed and be cast into the sea,' and does not doubt in his heart, but believes that those things he says will come to pass, he will have whatever he says. Therefore I say to you, whatever things you ask when you pray, believe that you receive them, and you will have them."' Clearly the 'mountains' of this promise are not the physical elevations which could be seen in almost any part of Palestine, but problems, difficulties, or human needs. Jesus teaches that any great burden which blocks our path should be brought to God in prayer and 'removed' by faith.

Jesus taught his disciples the importance of united prayer — prayer in concert: 'Again I say to you that if two of you agree on earth concerning anything that they ask, it will be done for them by my Father in heaven. For where two or three are gathered together in my name, I am there in the midst of them' (Matt. 18:19-20). We can see from the context that Jesus is speaking of the executive power of the gathered people of God to exercise discipline in their midst. When the church, after prayerful consideration, takes action to deal with wicked behaviour, what is bound on earth is also bound in heaven (v. 18). But undoubtedly it is also a general promise that God honours the prayers of his children when they agree together to pray for any worthy enterprise. Wherever God's children are, whatever their relationship is to each other, whatever their need may be, they should combine their minds and hearts and petition the Father. This is truly a 'threefold cord' that 'is not quickly broken' (Eccles. 4:12).

What an incentive and encouragement this promise is to the churches of Jesus Christ, even very small churches! If Jesus had said that the prayers of 10,000, agreeing together, would be heard, that would be a marvellous promise, but out of the reach of most

Christian groups. But he said that if but 'any two of you' unite in faithful prayer, the Father will give the blessing. Every congregation of believers which is seeking to preach the gospel of God's sovereign grace and make an impact on their community with the testimony of truth should frequently share and believe this promise. In fact any group of believers seeking to promote the gospel of Christ should appropriate this verse and claim the blessing it promises. Of course the primary application is to God's people in the covenant capacity of the local church. The local church is God's primary instrument for establishing his kingdom on earth.

The promise of power and blessing in united prayer certainly applies to believers, in at least a secondary way, at the domestic level. In a day of increasing family difficulties, when separations and divorce are only too commonplace, how important it is that husbands and wives join their hearts in prayer together! Next to Christians in church relationship there is no situation in which this promise is more relevant. Alienations and disagreements in the home can be solved when husband and wife 'agree' to bring their difficulties to God. Financial hardships and countless other trials and sorrows can be assuaged as those in the intimate family circle plead together at the throne of God's grace.

In John 15:7 we find another powerful prayer promise which connects power in prayer and *obedience*: 'If you abide in me, and my words abide in you, you will ask what you desire, and it shall be done for you.' This promise seems on the surface to be the proverbial *carte blanche* — the blank cheque. Jesus tells the disciples that they have only to ask and their desires will be fulfilled. Yet there is an important condition attached to this promise: it is the person who is 'abiding in Christ' who enjoys this blessing. While all believers, no doubt, are 'in Christ' by faith and through the indwelling of the Spirit, it is clear that intimacy with the Saviour admits of degrees. To abide in Christ means to be connected to him not only by our faith, but by the strong attachment of unquestioned fidelity and obedience. It means to be submitted to his will, dominated by his Word, filled with his Spirit. It stands to reason that the more a child of God is lifted above his own selfish and carnal pursuits, and devoted to the cause and claims of his sovereign Saviour, the more he is in a fit condition to be the recipient of God's choicest mercies.

John 15:7 is an amazing promise. It is almost as if Jesus is saying that the Spirit-filled Christian has sovereign authority in heaven. He can ask what he wills and it will be given to him. The scope of his blessings is limited only by his desires and faith. Yet the expression, 'if you abide in me,' is a restraint against a misapplication of the text. We do not have here an open invitation for anyone to get anything he or she wants from God. What person is likely to ask for the things God has planned to give? Clearly one who is living close to the heart of the Lord and walking in step with his purposes. Such a person will not be asking for things that do not honour the Lord. He will not be concerned primarily about his own petty schemes and ambitions, but will be praying for that which will glorify and magnify his Saviour. The believer who is abiding in Christ will not 'desire' carnal pleasure, but will set his sights on God's great plan. He can 'ask what he will', but what will he desire? He will desire the great blessings that God has promised. He will long for the accomplishments that bring glory to God and are for the good of the church as a whole. The Christian who is abiding in Christ is one chosen of God to be an instrument of dispensing his choicest mercies.

Praying in faith

All the lessons of Jesus Christ on prayer imply that faith is the key element. The parable of the persistent friend is designed specifically to teach that the believer who continues to seek blessings from God will prevail. In the 'ask, seek and knock' promise Jesus assures the disciples that earnest prayer will be successful. But a promise is only a key. If the door to the treasure room of heaven is opened, so to speak, the key must be used. When a safety rope is thrown to a man sinking in the waters, he must grasp it to be pulled to safety. Just so, the glorious promises of Scripture must be believed and acted upon if their benefits are to be enjoyed.

The Scriptures are absolutely clear that it is not just praying that brings down the blessings of heaven; it is praying in faith. The Christian life begins in an act of faith. Believing the gospel and trusting the Saviour who is presented in it brings salvation (Rom. 1:16). Paul's confidence in the promises of the gospel enabled him to say that he knew in whom he believed and was persuaded that God would keep that which he had committed to him (2 Tim. 1:12). The principle of faith applies just as definitely in the Christian's walk as it does to his conversion. He must live and walk by faith just as he was saved by faith in the first place.

To win spiritual victories in the Christian warfare we must bring God's promises to him in prayer and claim them. Jesus taught his disciples that faith which 'moves mountains' is faith which is guaranteed of success, because it is based on the immovable foundation of God's own veracity. It is the person who believes and expects his prayers to be answered who sees mountains move. Jesus demanded faith on the part of those who came to him personally for help. Jairus, the ruler of the synagogue, 'begged' the Lord Jesus to do something for his little daughter who was about to die (Mark 5:23). But that was not enough. Jesus admonished him to believe: 'He said to the ruler of the synagogue, "Do not be afraid; only believe"' (Mark 5:36). Jesus attributed to unbelief the inability of the disciples to fulfil their mission in casting out the devils from the epilectic child (Matt. 17:20).

Since faith is so essential to prayer we need to know what it is to pray in faith. This is a subject that needs to be explored, because there has been a good bit of confusion about it. First we need to know what praying in faith does *not* mean. It certainly does not mean that when a Christian expects a specific blessing from God it will necessarily come to him. Our Lord's promise in Mark 11:23-24 may seem to teach that on the surface, but it does not do so in reality. The ordinary experience of God's people contradicts the notion that confident expectation of an event guarantees its fulfilment. Times on end I have heard believers state dogmatically that a certain thing was going to happen in answer to prayer, and yet they were later disappointed because the anticipated event did not occur. Things we expect to take place sometimes simply do not.

Some believers seem to have a very mystical or intuitive concept of faith. It is a faith which is based on subjective feelings or impressions. I have often talked to Christians who were dogmatic that they were going to get what they asked from God. This can be illustrated by a typical conversation with such a person.

Let's say that Joe has a sick brother, Bill. A discussion with Joe might go something like this: 'I know my brother is going to get well — I just know it.' 'How do you know it?' 'Because God has revealed it to me — we have prayed earnestly and claimed the promises of God. God will not go back on his word.' 'Where in the Word has

God promised to heal your brother?' 'He says in the Bible that if we ask according to his will, he hears us. It is God's will that his people should not be sick. Therefore he has shown us that Bill will be healed.'

There is a great fallacy in Joe's reasoning, although obviously he is very sincere. His prayer has been earnest and his faith, at least in his own perception, is very real. On one thing, at least, he is correct. *Faith is believing the promises of God.* Faith is believing what God has revealed in Scripture. But the fact is that God has not revealed in Scripture that physical healing, or any other material blessing, will infallibly come in any given situation. The truth is that Joe is very presumptuous in his dogmatic opinion that his brother Bill will be healed. No one should believe something absolutely which God has not promised absolutely.

There are, however, some things which God has definitely revealed in the Word by promise. He has revealed that he will never forsake his children (Heb. 13:5). Any Christian can claim that promise by faith and rest on it. God has revealed that his people will never be subjected to a temptation which is too great for them to bear (1 Cor. 10:13). They can by faith claim this blessed promise. God has revealed that anyone who lacks wisdom can ask it from God and will definitely receive it (James 1:5). We do not need to wonder whether a prayer for wisdom will be answered. God has plainly said that he will give it to those who seek it.

Even when a Christian prays for things for which there is no definite promise there are undoubtedly some things he can believe. For one thing, he can believe that *God is a loving Father* and is deeply interested in his well-being. He can believe that God has often been pleased to give his children the specific things they ask. Of course, that is not the same thing as saying that the believer can know infallibly that God will give the specific thing he prays for. It is, however, a great encouragement. God is under no written contract in his Word to grant any specific answer to a request which has no promise attached to it. But the goodness of his nature and the pattern of answered prayer we find in Scripture, and out of Scripture as well, encourage us to hope expectantly that we will receive a favourable reception at the throne of grace.

The Christian can believe not only in the Father's goodness but also in his *wisdom*. He can believe without a shadow of a doubt that God knows best, and if the blessing he seeks from God is truly for the glory of God and is what he truly needs in this situation, God will give it to him. But he also will have to recognize that it is God's sovereign prerogative to withhold the specific request if he wishes. It takes faith to appropriate a specific promise of God, such as his absolute promise to give wisdom, and act upon it. But it also takes faith to trust the wisdom of God when he does not give us exactly what we wish. To believe in the love of God even when we are frustrated, or to believe in the wisdom of God when our schemes crumble requires as much trust, if not more, as claiming a specific promise of God.

Let us not forget that while in biblical history God usually gave people exactly what they asked for, there were exceptions. King David begged God to spare his little boy from impending death, but he died (2 Sam. 12:16-18). Paul pleaded with God three times that the painful, humiliating 'thorn in the flesh' be removed, but God instead simply gave him grace to bear it (2 Cor. 12:7-9). God's giving Paul grace to bear his trial shows that sometimes God answers prayer in a way different from what his people desire and expect.

Shortly after my wife and I married, I preached at a church in the state of Florida with the view to a call as pastor. Four other candidates also spoke. My wife and I prayed that God would open this door for us. We wanted very much to serve in a pastoral position. The situation looked hopeful. But when the vote was taken I came in second by a couple of votes. This was a bitter disappointment. I wondered why God had allowed me to travel such a long distance without success. Yet in a matter of a few months I was a candidate in Pennsylvania and received a unanimous call from the people whom I now serve. I have had a happy relationship in this church for twenty-five years. I know now that the location, the temperament of the people, and many other circumstances are much better suited to me than the Florida church would have been. Incidentally within about a year after I came to Pennsylvania I heard that the church in Florida had disbanded and the property was sold at an auction. God answered my prayer by giving me something better than I asked.

There is no doubt that some presumptuous ideas, sometimes even downright fanaticism, have been propounded under the theme of 'praying in faith'. Even true believers have mistaken strong impressions or hunches for faith. Hope, even wishful thinking, can be confused with faith. But there is another extreme which, in the religious communities I move in, is just as fallacious. In general it seems to me that Christians do not rise to the level of confidence, faith and expectation in prayer that the Word of God warrants. They do not have a great vision for the spread of the gospel and pray optimistically for God's blessings on his work. Without conflict, passion, or trauma, they simply retreat into the haven of 'the will of God'. They may have, perhaps, a few feeble desires for success in God's work, and occasionally say a prayer for the ongoing of the kingdom, but they know nothing of the travail that usually precedes great interventions of God. Instead of persisting in seeking God for the mercies they should desire, they are quickly discouraged and weakly say, 'Oh well, it was not God's will.'

The Scriptures generally, and certainly our Lord Jesus Christ specifically, encouraged passionate, bold, persistent, trusting prayer on the part of his people. He is much more willing to bless than we are to request blessings. Usually it is not 'submission to God' that prevents believers from charging the ramparts of heaven but indifference. Making all allowances for the fact that we must submit to God's sovereign will for us, conceding that not all of our prayers are answered in specifically the form we present them, still the general thrust of Scripture is overwhelmingly in the direction of confidence in prayer. The Lord invites us to come frequently, boldly, ambitiously, creatively and persistently to our heavenly Father and ask blessings from his throne. How precious and encouraging is his promise if we could only claim it: 'Ask, and it shall be given to you; seek, and you will find; knock, and it will be opened to you.' Most cases of barrenness and fruitlessness in the lives of Christians result from their neglect of bold, believing prayer. 'You do not have because you do not ask' (James 4:2).

11.
Power: prayer for the influence of the Holy Spirit

'If a son asks for bread from any father among you, will he give him a stone? Or if he asks for a fish, will he give him a serpent instead of a fish? Or if he asks for an egg, will he offer him a scorpion? If you then, being evil, know how to give good gifts to your children, how much more will your heavenly Father give the Holy Spirit to those who ask him!' (Luke 11:11-13).

The teaching given by the Lord on prayer ends in a glorious finale with an emphasis on the ministry of the Holy Spirit. The import of the passage quoted above, which forms the basis for this chapter, is that the gift of the Holy Spirit is the greatest blessing the believer can receive in this life. This is perhaps surprising. The Saviour emphasizes that God is a giving God, a God who responds in infinite mercy to his children who cry out to him. But what is the greatest gift? Not, as some might imagine or assume, some physical or material blessing, but the glorious Third Person of the Trinity, the Spirit, who came to take Jesus' place.

Christ seeks in every way possible to convince the disciples that they are praying to a loving, compassionate, generous heavenly Father. The *model* he gives, sometimes referred to as 'The Lord's Prayer,' demonstrates that. The *picture* or illustration of prayer, that of the persistent friend, proves it. The marvellous *promise*, 'Ask, and it shall be given you,' establishes it. Now Jesus appeals to the disciples' own sense of paternal love to encourage them to believe that God answers prayer. On that he rests his case. If believers cannot be convinced by this, they never will be convinced.

Evil parents give; a good heavenly Father gives even more

Although we do not know much about the family backgrounds of
the disciples, we know that some of them were fathers. Peter was
definitely married, for his mother-in-law is mentioned as one of the
first people Jesus healed (Mark 1:29-31). Probably he had children.
At any rate the disciples knew that there is no earthly relationship in
which such powerful feelings of affection and concern are experienced as that between a parent and child. Jesus speaks to them of
their love for 'their children'.

Jesus now uses this parent-child relationship as a powerful
foundation for faith in prayer. He reasons, justly as no one can
dispute, that it is highly unreasonable or even unthinkable that any
normal parent would turn away a child of his heart who comes and
asks for food, such as fish, bread, or an egg. Somewhere in the world
there might be a father or mother who would be so cruel as to turn
away a child in need. Few, however, have ever seen a real parent
send away a child with a stone when he asked for bread, or piteously
throw a repulsive reptile at him when he pleads for a fish.

Jesus recognizes, of course, that the parents to whom God has
entrusted little children are sinners. This is indicated in the phrase,
'If you then being evil, know how to give good gifts ...' These are
not flattering words, to be sure. Christ, who knows the human heart
perfectly, reminds even his own disciples that, though saved by his
grace, they are still evil. They were, no doubt, loving fathers, saved
and regenerated fathers at that. None the less, as they well knew,
each of them had a carnal and selfish side to his nature. Jesus credits
them, notwithstanding this fact, with sufficient humanity and paternal compassion to be responsive to a little child who cries for
help, especially when that child is their own flesh and blood. Now
the Lord draws them into the net of his logic. Clearly he is saying,
'If you who are selfish and carnal men love to bestow blessings on
your own sons and daughters, how much more will your Father in
heaven — who is not evil but perfect goodness itself — share his
infinite bounty with his sons who come to him to have their needs
met!' There is here a simple but powerful analogy between human
parental love and that of God. No one can escape the force of the
lesson here.

The significance of the promise before us, 'How much more will
your heavenly Father give the Holy Spirit,' is clarified when we

compare the form of the promise here with the one recorded in Matthew. Here the wording is similar but somewhat different: 'If you then, being evil, know how to give good gifts to your children, how much more will your Father who is in heaven give good things to those who ask him!' (Matt. 7:11). Matthew puts the promise of blessing in a rather general form: 'good things'. But Luke's account of the promise (obviously given on a different occasion) specifies not 'good things' but 'the Holy Spirit'. 'Good things,' to most of us, would suggest a vast host of comforts and conveniences, ministering to our temporal well-being. But let us see what Jesus has in mind. To Jesus Christ 'good things' can be summed up in 'the Holy Spirit'. In the gift of the Holy Spirit to the people of God, Jesus is bestowing the supreme and ultimate good.

Praying for the Holy Spirit

Jesus Christ is obviously showing his disciples that they are likely to receive what they are actually asking for. If they ask for blessings on a low level, they will get those blessings. But if they raise their level of prayer to a higher and more ambitious goal, they can expect that also. And what would be a very high goal in praying? What would be a great, glorious, tremendous blessing to pray for? The answer is: the Holy Spirit. Not only does Jesus Christ teach that praying for the Holy Spirit is an exalted form of prayer, he assumes that the disciples will be praying such a prayer: 'How much more will your heavenly Father give the Holy Spirit to those who ask him!' Jesus is saying that he expects that they will be asking for the Holy Spirit and that the Father will be giving the Spirit to them.

'Praying for the Holy Spirit' — this is a powerful theme, although within the church of Christ, it is a somewhat controversial one. It is generally understood among Christians, and rightly so, that whenever a person receives the gospel unto salvation the Holy Spirit takes up his dwelling-place in his or her heart. The New Testament teaches that the Holy Spirit is given personally and perpetually to those who are the heirs of salvation (John 14:16; Rom. 8:9). There is no doubt that the Spirit's indwelling is a privilege that is enjoyed in a much deeper and fuller way in the New Testament dispensation, primarily because the coming of the Holy Spirit in his fulness waited on the completion of the historical ministry of Jesus Christ (John 7:39).

Although the progressive unfolding of the revelation of God's redeeming mercy in the Scriptures includes, as part and parcel of it, the truth of the fuller manifestation of the Holy Spirit in the New Testament era, some have made a wrong deduction from this truth. They argue that the Old Testament believers were virtually without the ministry of the Holy Spirit altogether. Reasoning from these premises, they conclude that Jesus' promise of the blessing of the Holy Spirit in response to prayer is given to the disciples in an Old Testament context, and that praying for the Holy Spirit is out of place for Christians now. In other words, this scheme of teaching would regard the promise of Luke 11:13 as legalistic and irrelevant to the New Testament church. (The same viewpoint regards the whole Sermon on the Mount as relevant only to the nation of Israel, not to the church 'under grace'.)

Such teaching is extremely misguided. It is true that we do not find as much emphasis on the power and personal indwelling of the Spirit in the Old Testament. But it is a mistake to conclude that the Old Testament saints carried on their lives without the Spirit's ministry. If the Holy Spirit did not indwell the pre-New Testament believers why did David pray, 'Do not take your Holy Spirit from me'? (Ps. 51:11). Peter tells us that it was by the Holy Spirit dwelling *in* them (not, as some have said, *upon* them) that the Old Testament prophets testified beforehand of the sufferings of Christ (1 Peter 1:11).

Certainly those who are saved by God's grace should not engage in prayer for the *indwelling* of the Holy Spirit any more than they should pray for justification. Those are blessings which they enjoy by virtue of their union with Jesus Christ through faith. But they certainly can and should pray for *a fuller and more powerful manifestation of the Holy Spirit in their lives*. The New Testament makes it clear that the Holy Spirit occupies the body of the Christian like a temple (1 Cor. 6:19). But there are other aspects of the Spirit's ministry that not only admit of degrees of fulness, but also are conditional, based on the Christian's level of obedience and submission.

There are several activities of the Third Person of the Trinity mentioned in Scripture in which the believer's responsibility is addressed. For one thing, believers are commanded to *walk in the Spirit* (Gal. 5:16). Walking in the Spirit clearly means thinking, speaking and acting under the promptings of the indwelling Third

Person. The context shows that the Christian still has, as a part of his personality, 'the flesh', which strives against God's law. If the believer gives rein to this principle he will fall into the 'lust of the flesh', with all its sordid manifestations, as listed in Galatians 5:19-21. But when the Spirit of God has free rein in the heart, the 'fruit of the Spirit' will be manifested, such as love, joy, peace, long-suffering, etc. (Gal. 5:22). If the Christian cannot manifest these graces in his own strength, and if their development depends on the Spirit's power, then it stands to reason that he should pray that God's Spirit will come in freshness and fulness so that he can walk in his power.

Also the believer is commanded to *be filled with the Spirit:* 'And do not be drunk with wine, in which is dissipation; but be filled with the Spirit' (Eph. 5:18). Here is a clear command which is both negative and positive. The believer is not to be intemperate, that is intoxicated with alcoholic consumption. The positive command is just as imperative, however. The Christian is to be filled with the Spirit.

Without a question there is an analogy drawn here between the sinful practice of inebriation and the soul-exalting and beneficial experience of being filled with the Spirit. A person who is overcome with the power of strong drink is carried beyond himself, as it were, and exhibits behaviour which is not normal. In the same way a Spirit-filled Christian has a boldness, courage, joy and peace that are not natural. The original disciples, who cringed with fear before the Holy Spirit came in fulness and power upon them at Pentecost, 'spoke the word of God with boldness' after they 'were all filled with the Holy Spirit' (Acts 4:31). If the sovereign power of the Spirit is necessary for the power that the church needs in witnessing for Christ and experiencing the supernatural spiritual passion that is so contrary to frail human nature, then certainly believers need to pray for the filling of the Holy Spirit.

Finally, the Christian is commanded *not to grieve the Holy Spirit* (Eph. 4:30). Any intrusion into the life of the child of God, whether it be in the form of wicked thoughts, rash speech, or sinful deeds, grieves the holy God who dwells in the heart through his Spirit. Believers are responsible to walk in obedience to the commands of Christ and 'work out their salvation with fear and trembling'. But, humbling as this fact is, it is also true that they must rely upon the internal direction of the Holy Spirit to maintain a faithful walk. It is, after all, God who works in them 'to will and do for his good pleasure' (Phil. 2:13). The Christian is both responsible to the Spirit and yet dependent upon him at the same time. It is no inappropriate prayer for the believer to ask God so to move in his heart through his Spirit that he will not grieve him and quench his influence.

The Holy Spirit's power in the church

Most of our emphasis in this chapter so far has been directed to the responsibility of the individual Christian to the Holy Spirit. There is, however, a corporate aspect to the Holy Spirit's ministry which is definitely to be the object of the Christian's prayers. The teachings of Jesus relative to prayer in Luke 11 are given in a communal context. The early disciples made up the nucleus of the original church of Jesus Christ. They were saved by the grace of God individually, but they were gathered together in a fellowship of faith and service to God. The Holy Spirit was not only given to them as individual believers, but as the church, the body of Christ. While the body of the believer is called the temple of the Holy Spirit in 1 Corinthians 6:19, the church is called the temple of the Spirit in 1 Corinthians 3:16. Paul tells the church at Ephesus that they were 'a habitation of God in the Spirit' (Eph. 2:22).

The permanent indwelling of the Holy Spirit in the Christian is altogether consistent with the fact that there are degrees of influence of the Spirit based on the Christian's faith and yieldedness. The same principle applies in the Holy Spirit's corporate life in the church. A congregation of people who are truly saved, proclaim the gospel and observe God's ordinances as delivered in the New Testament, does, as a fact of divine endowment, have the Spirit of God among them. However, the level of power and blessing they enjoy in their midst depends on the extent to which the Spirit of God is honoured and obeyed. Scriptures, history and experience teach that there are times when the Holy Spirit is poured out in greater power. At such times, often referred to as revival, or awakening, not only do believers manifest more of the love, zeal and godliness that is their rightful obligation, but also there is a decided impact upon the community at large. As a rule, when the church as a whole is filled with the Spirit, many sinners are converted to Christ and added to the ranks of believers.

Church history abounds with examples of God's blessing the church with unusual manifestations of the power of the Holy Spirit in response to the prayers of believers. People even today read with amazement the account of the marvellous spiritual transformations that took place in Great Britain and the American colonies during what has been called the Great Awakening. What is not generally known, however, is the preparatory work of prayer which preceded this transformation.

There is at the present time a revival of interest in the theology and ministry of Jonathan Edwards. It is finally being recognized that not only was he the greatest philosophical mind of North America, but he was actually one of the spiritual founders of the American nation. One of his greatest works was his *Humble Attempt to Promote Explicit Agreement and Visible Union of God's People in Extraordinary Prayer*. In this he calls upon believers everywhere to plead with God for an outpouring of the Holy Spirit upon the church. The results of such a strategy can be seen in the effects of the awakening he witnessed in his parish at Northampton, Massachusetts.

One of the most remarkable awakenings ever known in the United States was the great revival of 1857. It began in a little room in the lower part of the city of New York on the third floor of the Dutch Reformed Church on Fulton Street. It was here that a 'downtown' missionary named Jeremiah Lamphier began some noon prayer meetings. The specific purpose of these meetings was to pray for a spiritual awakening. At first there were only three persons, then six, twenty and finally the building was unable to accommodate the crowds which came. The spiritual energy which was generated in this simple beginning spread throughout New York and eventually to Philadelphia, Boston and other cities and towns, until eventually few places in the United States were without such meetings. Out of this came a powerful revival which was reported in secular newspapers and broadcast by telegraph throughout the world.[1]

Frankly I find among believers today a good bit of scepticism regarding the possibility of revival in our own day. Sometimes this seems to originate in a conviction that the 'end of the world' is upon us and that we are now in the final great apostasy. This was illustrated vividly to me a quarter of a century or so ago when I was ministering in a little mission church in central Kentucky. I had

called on the people in my church to pray for spiritual awakening
and had invited a guest minister for several days. One evening as we
were standing in front of the church a gentleman spoke to the
evangelist and myself and chided us for raising hopes for repentance, revival and reformation in the church today. 'We are,' he said
confidently, 'living in the days of gleanings from the fields. The
great harvest of souls is over. There will never be another spiritual
awakening in our land. These are the "last days", during which,
according to the Scriptures, times will get steadily worse.' What he
was saying, in effect was, 'Don't waste your time calling on
believers to turn from their sins and seek God for revival. It is
useless.'

Here is a case of a gross misapplication of Scripture. It is true that
the Bible teaches that towards the end of the age times of terrible
apostasy will take place and evil men will wax worse and worse. But
it is a grave mistake to allow prophetic speculation to rob Christians
of the benefits of plain promises of the Word of God. Neither this
gentleman nor anyone else can say dogmatically where we are in the
final scheme of things. He may be right; we may be living in the
period of time before Jesus returns. Perhaps some good can take
place when people believe this. If watching for Jesus' return causes
believers to be more zealous in evangelism and more earnest in
prayer, it is a practical truth. But when it is used to spread fatalistic
pessimism in the ranks of those who are seeking to bring about
spiritual reformation, the truth of Jesus' return is being distorted. No
one knows the day or hour in which the Saviour will come back to
earth. What we do know for sure is that God wants his people to seek
his face, turn from their sins and plead for the power of the Holy
Spirit. The promise of Luke 11:13 that God will give the power of
the Spirit to those who ask cannot be annulled by theories as to God's
prophetic timetable.

There is much for which we can be thankful as Christians about
what God is doing in his kingdom as we near the twenty-first
century. On the apologetic front, the arguments of the sceptics about
the credibility of the Scriptures and the gospel they proclaim are
successfully being met. There seems to be a growing hunger among
believers for more solid doctrinal instruction and a growing ap-
preciation of the great heritage we have in the evangelical faith. All
of this is not enough, however. Sound philosophical arguments,
correct doctrinal interpretations and even clear and interesting

preaching and teaching are not sufficient. We need a fresh outpouring of the Holy Spirit upon the church today. It is his presence in the church that removes the lethargy and boredom that so frequently plagues even the best of Christians. It is his mighty influence that gives success to the preaching of the Word and brings the lost to salvation.

This is a fitting place to close this study on prayer, as taught by Jesus Christ himself. Of all the mercies we need to pray for most, the Holy Spirit must certainly come at the top. Believers not only need to ask God for the Spirit's blessings on the ministrations of the gospel, but by faith to claim God's gracious promise that he will give to those who ask: 'And I say to you, ask, and it will be given to you; seek, and you will find; knock, and it will be opened to you. For everyone who asks receives, and he who seeks finds, and to him who knocks it will be opened' (Luke 11:9-10). There has been no change in God's plan for awakening and reformation in the church. The same Jesus who ascended on high 2,000 years ago and sent his Spirit down upon the waiting church will bestow this spiritual power today if we truly want it and plead for it.

A. W. Tozer once said in a lecture to Christian college students that when we *desire* a blessing and pray for it we may very well get it. When we are *determined* to receive a blessing from God and pray for it we probably will get it. But when we are *desperate* for a blessing from God we surely will get it. Whether God's people are desperate yet for a spiritual awakening is uncertain. But the needs of our generation are desperate. The church generally is in a desperate condition of compromise and lukewarmness. May God give to us such holy strivings for the Spirit's power that we are desperate in our urgencies of prayer. May we say like Jacob of old, 'I will not let you go unless you bless me.'

1. An excellent account of the 'Fulton Street Prayer Revival' is found in Warren A. Candler, *Great Revivals and the Great Republic* (1904).